WALL STREET SCANDALS

WALL STREET SCANDALS

Greed and trading on Wall Street
The American Way

Winston Overton

Copyright © 2013 by Winston Overton.

Library of Congress Control Number:		2012924271
ISBN:	Hardcover	978-1-4797-7250-6
	Softcover	978-1-4797-7249-0
	Ebook	978-1-4797-7251-3

All rights reserved. No part of this book may be reproduced or transmitted in any form or by any means, electronic or mechanical, including photocopying, recording, or by any information storage and retrieval system, without permission in writing from the copyright owner.

This book was printed in the United States of America.

To order additional copies of this book, contact:
Xlibris Corporation
1-888-795-4274
www.Xlibris.com
Orders@Xlibris.com

Contents

AUTHOR BIOGRAPHY 9
DEDICATION 11
BOOK DESCRIPTION 13

CHAPTER ONE

THE ESTABLISHMENT OF THE
CAPITAL TRADING EXCHANGE 15

    TRADING FLOOR COMMUNICATIONS 19
    THE CAPITAL TRADING EXCHANGE AS AN SRO 22
    THE CTE EARLY ORGANIZATION CHART 23
    CASES OF INJUSTICES AT THE CTE 26
    EDWIN MANSFIELD—WHISTLEBLOWER 28
    THE INFORMANT OF THE CTE 29
    REPORTERS ON THE CTE TRADING FLOOR 31
    POST SUPERVISORS ON THE CTE TRADING FLOOR 31
    THE SUITS 32
    RELIGIOUS LIBERTY AT THE CTE 33
    BROKER/MEMBERS 33
    THE SPECIALIST RESPONSIBILITIES 34
    TRADING OPTIONS 35
    THE FEEL GOOD MOTTO 36
    THE CAPITAL TRADING EXCHANGE
    OPERATING SYSTEM 36

CHAPTER TWO

AGENCIES THAT INFLUENCE THE STOCK MARKETS 41

- THE SECURITIES AND EXCHANGE COMMISSION 41
- SEC FORMATION: 41
- SEC INVESTIGATIVE WORK 42
- SEC DETECTION TO PROSECUTION 43
- THE FEDERAL RESERVE 45
- CONGRESSIONAL ACTIONS—NCFRR 47
- DODD—FRANK WALL STREET REFORM 49

CHAPTER THREE

HOLDING ACCOUNTANTS ACCOUNTABLE 51

- AUTOMOTIVE INDUSTRY CRISIS OF 2008-2010 55
- TARP-CONGRESS AUTHORIZES THE TREASURY DEPARTMENT 57
- REGIONS RETURNS TARP MONEY 61
- INSIDER TRADING 61
- INSIDER BILL PASSES WITH NEW BACKERS 63
- BAN ON INSIDER TRADING BY CONGRESS BECOMES LAW 64
- INVESTORS—BEWARE OF PRE-IPO SECONDARY MARKETS 65
- FACEBOOK SHARES START TRADING 67
- GOLDMAN PLAYS DAMAGE CONTROL 68
- OCCUPY WALL STREET—2011 70
- BBA LIBOR 71

CHAPTER FOUR

EXCERPTS ON THE GREED OF BANKERS
AND TRADERS ON WALL STREET 74

    ENRON CORPORATION—BANKRUPTCY 75
    CITICORP SETTLEMENT—FRAUD CHARGES 78
    CHARLES H. KEATING—
    VIOLATION OF SECURITIES LAW 80
    MICHAEL MILKEN—JUNK-BOND FELONIES 80
    IVAN BOESKY—INSIDER TRADING 81
    LEHMAN BROTHERS 83
    BERNARD MADOFF—PONZI SCHEME 86
    ALLEN STANFORD—PONZI SCHEME 94
    WELLS FARGO BANK—RIGGING OF TRANSACTIONS 97
    PHILIP FALCONE—FRAUD CHARGES 97
    AMERICAN INTERNATIONAL GROUP—(AIG) 99
    SOLYNDRA—(SCANDAL AND BANKRUPTCY) 103
    THE SOLAR SECTOR—GONE BELLYUP 105
    MF GLOBAL—(JON CORZINE) 107
    RAJ RAJARATNAM, HEDGE FUND BILLIONAIRE 114
    RAJAT GUPTA—SECURITIES FRAUD 117
    ANIL KUMAR—INSIDER TRADING 121
    TOM PETTERS—FRAUD CHARGES 123
    FANNIE MAE AND FREDDIE MAC—
    SUBPRIME MORTGAGES 126
    SUIT OVER MORTGAGE BONDS 128
    SEC UPS GAME TO FIND ROGUE FIRMS 129
    SEC EASES REPORTING FOR AUDITS OF TRADING 132
    INSIDER TRADING PROBE AT SEC—SCANDALOUS 133
    JAMIE DIMON 134

CHAPTER FIVE

MAJOR INVESTIGATION OF SCANDAL AT AMEX 137

- A PROPOSITION REVEALED ON A MERGER 138
- CREATING A GLOBAL MARKET 140
- THE NASD DEAL 141
- DISAPPOINTMENT AND DISPLEASURE 142
- THE PARTING OF THE WAVES 143
- PHILADELPHIA EXCHANGE TO MERGE
  WITH NASDAQ & AMEX 144
- NASD AND THE NYSE FUED OVER AMEX 146
- THE AMEX AS CHEAP STREET 149
- THE AMEX AS A COMPETITIVE EXCHANGE (SRO) 150
- NYSE EURONEXT TO ACQUIRE AMEX 151
- BIBLIOGRAPHY 154
- INDEX ....

Author Biography

Winston Overton was born in Georgetown, British Guiana, South America: now independently known as "The Cooperative Republic of Guyana". He is the eldest child followed by a brother—Aubrey Overton of Georgetown Guyana, and a sister—the late Sgt. Shirley Overton-Campbell of New Amsterdam, Berbice, Guyana: from the union of the late Randolph Overton and Nova Eslyn Overton. His dad also fathered other younger siblings in Wismar, Guyana. He boasts of having had the best Grandmother one could ever have asked for—Mrs. Miriam Waldron. His Mom now deceased, was his Queen Of Hearts and often boasted that she had the best mother-in-law in Miriam Waldron one could ever have asked for.

Winston was a former employee in the drawing offices of the Hydrographic and Sea Defense Department of the Ministry of Works and Hydraulics in Kingston, Georgetown, Guyana; and The Geological Survey Department, Brickdam, Georgetown, Guyana; before accepting a contract as a Cartographer with the Government of the Republic of Zambia, Central Africa—a country he was proud to call his second home.

At the end of that contract with the Government of Zambia, Winston travelled extensively throughout Africa and Europe before migrating to the United States. He worked at Chase Manhattan Bank and Manufacturers Hanover Trust Bank, in the late 1970s before joining the staff of the American Stock Exchange: finally retiring in 2002.

DEDICATION

    This book is dedicated to my only loving Son—Kwame Adam Overton, a Son that anyone would be proud to call their own. With dedication and love to my grandchildren, Johnathan Ethan Overton, Mariah Hannah Overton, Elaysha Bazil, and Elijah Reid; who are the gems in my crown.

    Special acknowledgement goes to my stepdaughter June Ann Joaquin, who lauds me with telephone calls of respect and best wishes on special occasions.

"For wisdom is a defense, and money is a defense:
But the excellency of knowledge is,
that wisdom gives life to them that have it."
ECL: 7, V12

Book Description

    This book is a compilation of collective intellectual properties, along with the author's interpolations. It presents to the reader, the historical birth of the Capital Trading Exchange (CTE); and also throws light on the corporate greed of Executives on Wall Street, here in the United States: which now echoes concerns for Private Investors, Senior Citizens, and the Middle Class throughout the world, thus in part, causing the spread of the "Occupy Wall Street Movement", which will be discussed in a later chapter.

    Though this book was not written in strict chronological order, it is factual. The Author was a former employee of the financial district and very familiar with the Stock Exchanges and their operations. Also covered is the American Stock Exchange (known as the AMEX aka "cheap street".) He has offered a brief overview of the CTE's birth, a glimpse of its operational systems, growth, administrative ineptitudes, scandalous episodes and the imminent demise of both the CTE and the AMEX. The names of flawed characters have been changed to hide their identity. Some of the information provided is just the tip of the iceberg. Worldwide Investors, High School Seniors and College Students should all be able to glean from this book a good introductory reading into the wiles of Wall Street.

    These are the actions of greedy executives that culminated in the formation of the "Occupy Wall Street Movement", the need for the "Dodd-Frank Wall Street Reform Act", the increased vigilance of the "Securities and Exchange Commission", and increased prosecutions. This kind of contemptible behavior is apparent worldwide; as we can see from the BBA-Libor scandal.

    It is hoped that by investors reading this book, they will heed warnings that novices who want to play the Stock Market will invest only what they can afford to lose without crying. The author suggests that you use your play money intelligently. As you read this book perhaps you will see the need to study the Stock Markets, learn to use Charts and Graphs, and get the services of a qualified Financial Advisor before investing—hopefully you can find an honest one. Investors—Caveat Emptor.

- ❖ Susan Shapiro warns, "Middle-class pensioners commit their life savings to a company that purports to have developed the technology to turn sand and gravel into gold." (Shapiro, Wayward Capitalists, 1984) 1

Chapter One

THE ESTABLISHMENT OF THE CAPITAL TRADING EXCHANGE

The Capital Trading Exchange, (CTE) existed as part of the New York Curb Market, which conducted business at its open air quarters on Broad Street, Lower Manhattan in 1908, and was registered as the Capital Trading Exchange in 1912. The Capital Trading Exchange was the third largest Stock and Options trading exchange in the New York Financial District.

The brokers of the Capital Trading Exchange, were originally known as part of the Curbstone Brokers, because they traded in the street; those equities that did not meet the listing requirements of the New York Stock Exchange. Additionally, around that time, the New York Stock Exchange would only permit trading companies that had at least one hundred registered stocks to trade indoors at their facility. A number of years passed by, after which the curbstone brokers moved indoors to their own facilities in lower Manhattan in 1922 and was renamed the Capital Trading Exchange. The CTE was always the youngest, drug-addicted and alcoholic aspiring stepsister to the New York Stock Exchange. This ambitious stepsister always tried to emulate her big sister by adopting her regulatory policies, and always looked up to the New York Stock Exchange for leadership when it came to major decisions. For example, when it came to decisions of earlier trading hours and early closings, the CTE followed the NYSE's lead.

The Curbside Brokers officially moved into their then impressive six-storey indoor Trading Facility on June 29, 1922; a stone's throw from the NYSE on Broad Street. The building at the time was erected to create a similar atmosphere to the outdoor facility, allowing a small portion of the building to be used for offices and a Boardroom for the Governors, while maintaining high ornate ceilings to give that open-air feeling. The facade and office entrance was not as impressive as its competitor—The New York Stock Exchange, but was modern by the architectural standards of those days.

When the building was first erected, it stood six stories high; then in 1931 construction of new office space brought a newer and bolder look of a fourteen-story ultra-modern building. Thereafter, The Curb Exchange became known as the Capital Trading Exchange. However, because office staff at the Administrative level became extremely top heavy; *(known as the suits)* a decision was made to purchase and annex the adjoining building.

After years of ownership the clever executives at the CTE along with the Board of Governors decided to sell the adjoining building and remain as tenants. Perhaps the CTE was in a financial bind at the time and needed a boost. Just how wise a decision it was at that time is a financial blunder, now dead and buried. As time passed and the enormous payout for rent was realized, these clever entrepreneurs made a final decision to repurchase the building at an inflated price, according to reliable sources.

As for selecting the Financial / Educational Institution those folks attended for their academia, please don't go there and waste money on your tuition. No one may be excited about hiring you to implement similar tactics to their establishment. In today's business environment, there is no tolerance for trial and error.

Since the original building of The Capital Trading Exchange was originally erected side by side with the newly annexed building, which shared a common wall, it was decided that the two buildings should be made more accessible to each other. On the ground floor of the annexed building sizable opening was made to give access to the main Trading Floor of the CTE; and to the bank of elevators that led to the Executive Offices. Two spaces were allotted on the ground floor of annexed building for rental to a Chinese Restaurant and a small Burger Joint (what one would by today's standards call a small "Greasy Spoon". Additionally, a doorway was cut at the eight floor of the original building which connected to the sixth floor of the annexed building that gave easy access to the Security and Microfiche Offices.

On the ground floor of the CTE, space for rental was made available for a restaurant named "Sammy's at the Capital Trading Exchange" A proposed upscale eatery principally for Brokers and their Guests.

By today's standards in New York City, that eatery would have had numerous Health Code Violations. The floors in the kitchen were dirty and mucky, and often times, large rats (almost the size of squirrels) were often seen scurrying across the kitchen floor; which was visible to trading floor staff as they passed by the open kitchen doors. "Sammy's at the CTE" was reputed to have cuisines of a high culinary standard—so said those who ate there—and that the prices were reasonable. The major source with rat infestation emanated from the Trading Floor one level above "Sammy's Restaurant". The problem was compounded by the Traders and various staff who left large portions of uneaten food around the work areas, which were taken by these large rodents under the elevated sub-floors that housed the communications cables, tube carriers, and electrical cables, etc. But what would New York be without huge rats—rodents and humanoids alike?

On the Trading Floor, communications, electronics, and organization in the 1970s through the late 1980s were not as advanced as in later years. The trading posts were originally circular in construction, housing a combination of stock and option overhead display-screens. Chalk boards for displaying stock volumes, with their bids and offers, and position books were the norm of the day, displayed on the available counter space. Pneumatic tubes and conveyor belts with small plastic tube-carriers were used to send execution orders to and from the posts and sub-stations, sorted by data clerks, and walked over to the relative broker companies by the floor runners; to inform the companies of the status of their orders.

Electronic Card Readers and Marked-Sensed Cards were used by the Reporters to communicate trades and quotes to Traders and Investors, and to the world at large.

These are examples of "Marked Sensed Cards" that were once used by the American Stock Exchange to process executed stock trades and quotes. Note that Stocks first traded in eights of a dollar prior to the year 2001, after which stock prices were decimalized for simplicity, promoting investor confidence, and keeping abreast with the other major exchanges; local and foreign.

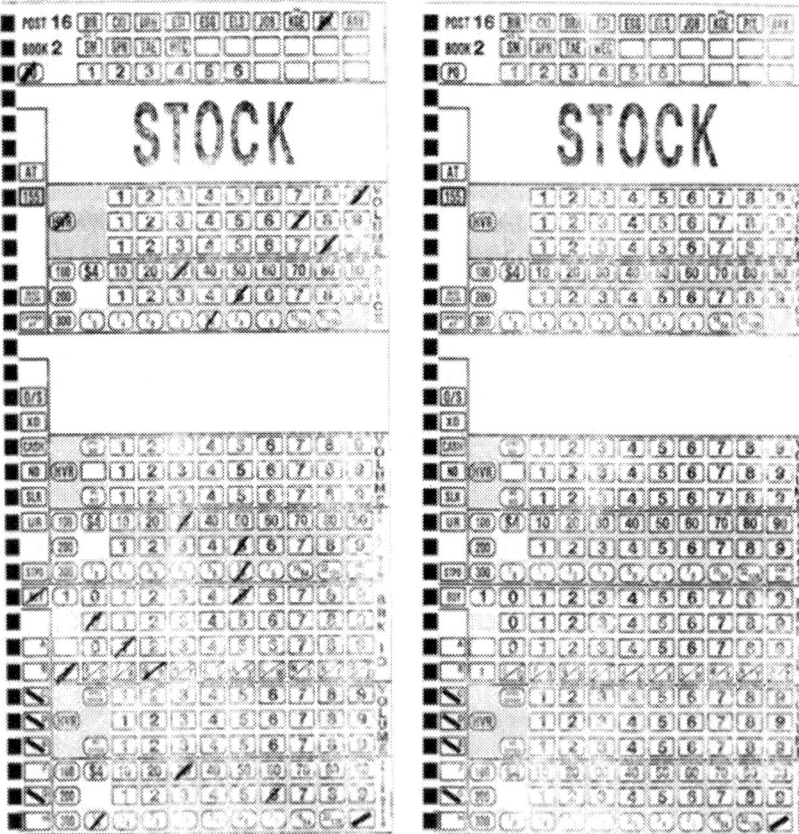

(1) Traded 978 PIX @ $35 5/8
(2) Bid 35 3/4 – Offer 36 1/8
    Broker I.D. #5015

Blank Card.

Unfortunately, examples of all marked sensed cards that were used on the Capital Trading Exchange are no longer available, except for the Stock Cards which demonstrates trades and quotes that were marked by the Reporters and ready for the Data-Clerks to place in the electronic card readers and time stamped.

Note that Stocks and Options were originally traded in fractions of a Dollar (e.g. Sixteenths and eights) and later the CTE changed over to a decimal system to keep abreast with other Exchanges and International Trading.

TRADING FLOOR COMMUNICATIONS

Cellular phones and land lines were not permitted to be used then for communications between Floor Brokers and their Clerks manning their individual booths. Mounted on the northern and southern walls of the Trading Floor high above all, were two huge electronically lit boards with numbers representing each broker or the Broker Firm. Whenever a number was lit up the corresponding broker would yell out to his clerk and a series of hand signals (similar to American Sign Language) would be used to communicate purchase orders and confirm executed trades, and or gave quotes.

Eventually, telephone kiosks were erected across the floor. Telephone lines were activated in the clerical booths; and additionally beepers were worn by the brokers so that they can be alerted in very vociferous trading crowds if they were needed by their individual companies. As a result, the lighted Communications Boards became obsolete and were dismantled. Gradually hand signals became a thing of the past as electronic communications took precedent, in an ever growing technologically advancing marketplace.

In an article that was put out by the Capital Trading Exchange, it was expressed that primary to the concept of the auction market they represent, is the opportunity for all traders and the investors they represent to have and achieve the best price available. However, a lot of illegal activities were prevalent back then as later. Greed was the order of the day. At the heart of this system was the fact that public orders were supposed to be given priority. Unlike the over-the-counter market, the Capital Trading Exchange was not driven by professional dealers; who were often allowed to trade for their own accounts ahead of the public. Public order priority means better and fairer pricing for investors because there is no 'middle man' markup caused by dealer intervention. The Specialists' mandates were to maintain a fair and orderly market at all times.

The business of trading has always been fast paced. From the beginning, when CTE brokers worked outdoors, ambition and competition demanded an edge. All brokers were well decked out in suits before they started to work indoors, but soon wore blue and white striped smock-jackets, and later in order to be seen quickly by their clerks in a crowded marketplace, each company adopted their own colors with their company acronyms emblazoned. To communicate consummated transactions a series of intelligent hand signals were developed, since the overhead Electronic Ticker Tapes were not yet introduced. There was an old system that used paper tape, which was loaded up and made ready before trading begun each day. That was where the Brokers went for missing information, whether it was about trade executions or Reuters News. That was then, but later hand signals were rarely used, as Beepers were given to the Brokers, and a number of Kiosks were strategically placed around the Trading Floor; each Kiosk carried ten telephones for communications between the Brokers and their Clerks, and two electronic monitors for monitoring trading activities. The CTE saw the importance of being more technologically advanced in competition with other Exchanges and sought to improve all aspects of an innovative Stock Exchange, and sought further to create more trading floor area to accommodate new listings.

Additionally, another trading floor was constructed on the second floor of the annexed building called the "Blue-room"; and yet another trading floor was designed and constructed on the entire ground floor of the original building, which originally housed "Sammy's at the Capital Trading Exchange".

In July of 1993, technology went a step further, when an experimental hand-held computer was introduced to the floor brokers. These small computers were introduced in order to speed up trade entries unto the Specialist Electronic Books for execution. Previously, the Trader/Broker would write their trades on Buy or Sell Order Tickets, and submitted to the Specialist Clerks. The orders would then be tallied with a bid and offer size and announced to the trading crowd. During the time that the Clerks took to enter the orders onto the Electronic Books, electronically matched orders would be executed, thus trading through legitimately timed-clocked orders. This caused a lot of confusion, complaints and trading reconciliation during trading hours and in the DK Room (Don't Know Room) the following morning. As is well known, change is not always easily acceptable by all. After a period of time, practically all the Brokers accepted the change for a small hand-held computer, except for one senior Broker. In 1993 that broker was about 80 years old, with a mind as sharp as a tack, and with health and energy to match that of a much younger man than himself. Believe it or not, he was able to match his calculation speed and accuracy with the younger men on their computers.

At 80 plus years, that broker was still trading on the Capital Trading Exchange, holding on to the rails and swinging up and down the escalators from one Trading Floor to the other; (of which there were four floors namely—the main floor, mezzanine, blue-room, and ground floor). He loved dancing and was very strict when it came to observing the rules on the floor, though at times he was an agitated complete nuisance.

Sadly, he lost his son on 09/11/01 when the World Trade Center Towers collapsed. That day will live in infamy, as two well respected and adored brokers; Eustace Rudy Bacchus and Michael J. Pascuma Jr., were attending a breakfast meeting on "Windows of the World"—WTC. In honor of these two men and as a loving memorial, the following photographs are presented. Heartfelt condolences go out to all who have lost their loved-ones and friends in the terrorist attack of the World Trade Center.

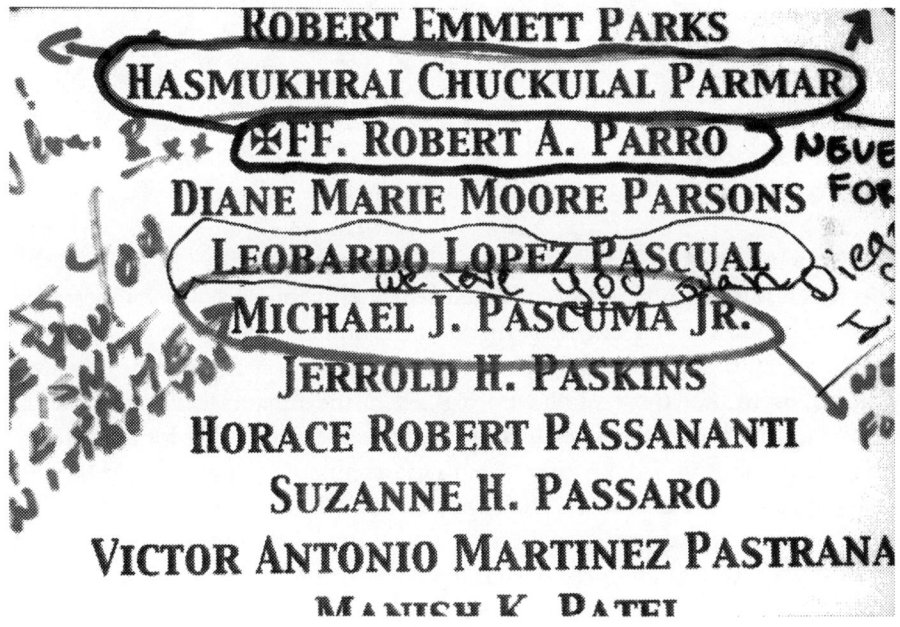

PASCUMA JR.
DIED—WTC—09/11

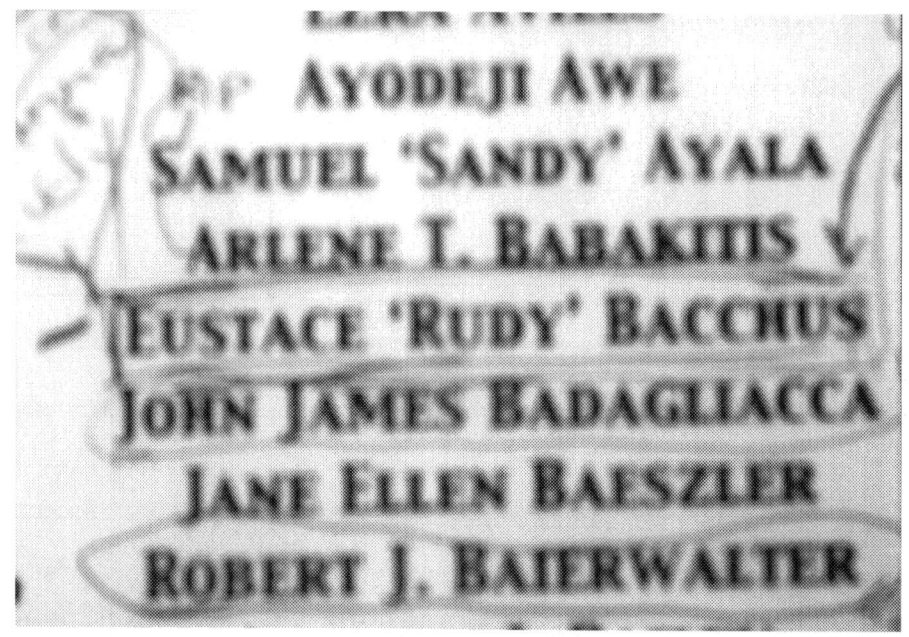

RUDY BACCHUS
DIED—WTC—09/11

As a result of the 9/11 disaster, extensive security measures were undertaken by The Capital Trading Exchange, including criminal background checks on all employees of the CTE and member-firm staff. Life was never the same after that sad event. For those of us who worked in the Financial District—it was nerve racking. The smell of death permeated the air all around us for quite a long period of time. Every day, workers and visitors alike to the area could be seen wearing surgical masks or covering their noses with their handkerchiefs. The sight was very depressing, appetites for breakfast, lunch and snacks were lost, and the CTE brought in medical staff to help evaluate and refer members of the staff for treatment in dealing with their psychological traumatic experiences.

THE CAPITAL TRADING EXCHANGE AS AN SRO

The Capital Trading Exchange book on its Constitution and Rules were many and complex because of more voluminous and complex trading. Their Constitution and Rules were necessary to maintain a fair and orderly auction market especially since the CTE was a Self-Regulatory Organization (SRO). When the CTE was just an outdoor marketplace at the inception—the members and staff had trading rules to observe. Some trading rules were established since the year 1911 but over the years stricter and more formal rules were implemented by its board of governors and exchange executives; especially after they started to trade indoors in the year 1922.

After trading began indoors the CTE had sought to adopt and mimic most of the rules and procedures of its most senior (SRO) competitor—the New York Stock Exchange also well known as the Big Board. The proposed function of the CTE as an SRO was to review trading, monitor activities of its members, and investigate reported infractions and to prosecute the violators. As with any SRO the CTE was mandated by the SEC to take disciplinary action against all violators. However, this did not always occur, since some heads of member firms were on the board of governors, and were the violators themselves. As such, decisions reached on the violators were often lop-sided. Some of the biggest concerns and practices determined to be infractions was that of insider trading, market manipulations, illegal trade activities, failure by the Specialists to maintain a fair and orderly market, and breaking other floor regulations, etc.

The CTE was usually alerted to rule violations through customer complaints, queries from listed companies, market surveillance, tips from floor members, integrated audit trail, referrals and recommendations from the SEC etc. The departments involved in self-regulation were trading analysis/equities, trading analysis/options, trading analysis/derivatives, and compliance and surveillance. Compliance and Surveillance embodied attorneys, trading analysis, sales practice representatives, financial examiners, stock watch, options watch, and enforcement. The legal and regulatory department helped to set up new policy proposals from the SEC that monitored legislation. Self-regulation was supposed to be a daily and an essential part of the successful operation at the Capital Trading Exchange. The market surveillance analysts were the CTE's detectives who investigated the reasons for activities. If violations occurred, hearings were set up for arbitration proceedings. Under the National Securities Markets Improvement Act of 1996, the Securities and Exchange Commission (SEC) was permitted to levy a fee on these SROs according to a percentage of the total dollar value of securities traded. These fees were implemented so as to offset the costs incurred by the government in supervising the officials of the Securities and Exchange Commission (SEC). Membership fees charged were also a source for meeting the levied SRO fees payable to the SEC.

THE CTE EARLY ORGANIZATION CHART

Even in the early stages of its operation, the Capital Trading Exchange always strived to be recognized as the "Preferred Auction Marketplace." The Organization Chart was presented to impress listing companies, that they were by no means a small operation and that the CTE could measure up to the biggest and the best. After the first Chart was presented and years went by, the Organization Chart got even larger and especially top-heavy with top earning executives. The quest for new products began, listing standards were lowered to entice companies, and for a while the CTE seemed to be on the way to major success and a promising and sustained future.

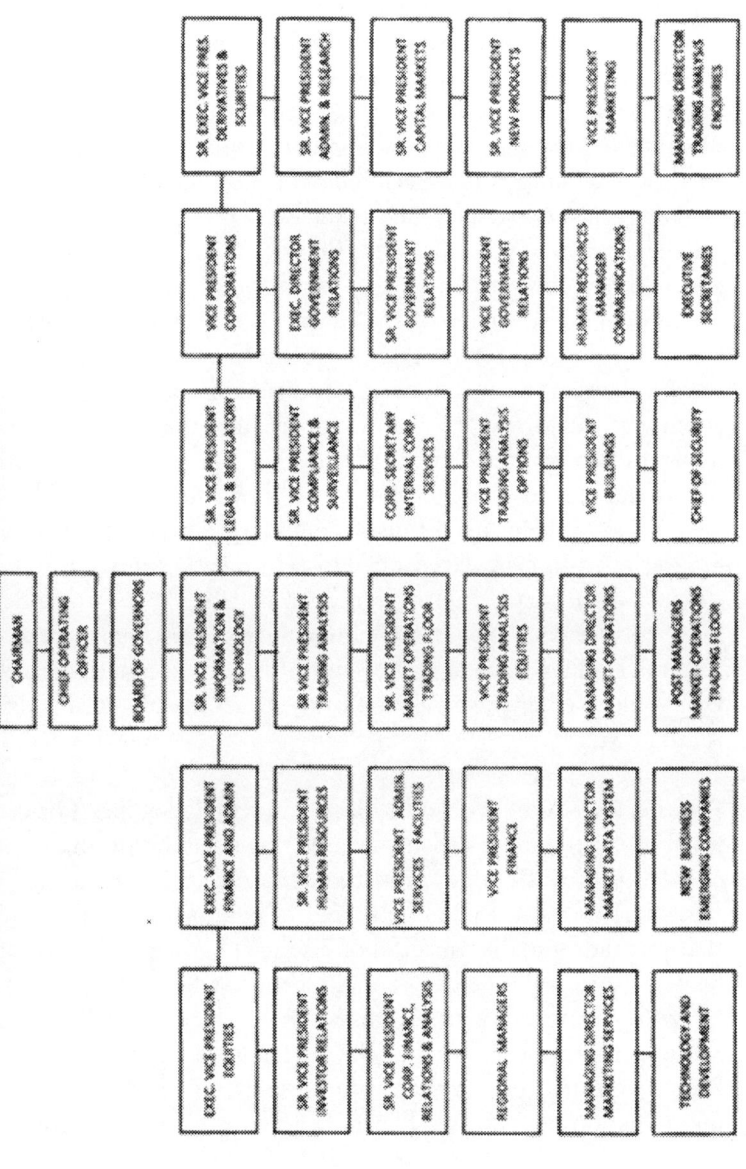

CASES OF INJUSTICES AT THE CTE

❖ The names of flawed characters portrayed in the following articles of this chapter, are either omitted or changed to protect their identities. Though there are many such cases, only the following incidents will be reported.

(1) One of the top cops in the trading analysis department of the Capital Trading Exchange was a black fellow Mike Richards, who was highly revered by just about everyone at the exchange, and especially by floor officials and floor governors. He started at the bottom of the ladder and climbed his way up to the top through hard work, merit, and his thorough knowledge of the rules and regulations. His experience spanned a period of more than 25 years. In spite of this, according to reliable sources, he was accused of not being knowledgeable enough about the rules and regulations governing the exchange and was unceremoniously discharged. What a heap of malarkey, and why did it take decades to establish that he did not know his job? Those who were responsible for his dismissal could have, at the least used another excuse, not this bare faced lie. This episode was among others that supported the many injustices perpetrated by the Iron Maiden that made all the decisions at the Human Resources Department of the Capital Trading Exchange. Because of lack of access to an interview with Mike Richards verification of the exact reasons for his dismissal is unknown.

(2) Another incident involved a black Human Resources Officer, who was constantly addressed in negative racist terms by the same Iron Maiden that was employed as the Senior Vice President of Human Resources at the CTE. He objected to being addressed in a manner that was rude and disrespectful of his racial heritage. He was told that he was too thin skinned and should learn to take a joke. Subsequently, he was threatened with dismissal. After hiring legal counsel and challenging the intentions of the exchange, a decision was made to keep everything hush-hush by offering him an undisclosed amount of money as compensation; if he would accept to resign his position. The settlement was attractive, and since he no longer desired to continue his employment with the CTE: he gracefully left with his head held high.

(3) It was reported in a New York newspaper that a sexual harassment charge brought by a female broker on the Capital Trading Exchange went unpunished. In fact the trader believed that management did not lend much credence to the facts she had presented. Ms. Ben, the female trader, was a very intelligent, successful and polite individual who won the hearts of many, male and female alike.

Because of the inaction of the CTE Management, Ms. Ben contemplated taking action in court against Mr. Scumbag—the male trader whom it was reported sexually harassed her on her arrival at the CTE in March 1999 and continued on several occasions until October 2000.

It is not known whether the court documents were filed, after the many frustrating discussions she had with the CTE legal staff. And if indeed there was a court proceeding, what was the outcome. No attempt will be made to elaborate on the purported actions of Mr. Scumbag, since not all the facts were made known publicly. Contrary to what was reported, Ms. Ben was not the first female black trader to work on the CTE, and it is not believed that she would hold claim to such. It was hoped that the reporter did not interject this claim in order to discredit the rest of her story.

On the other hand, Mr. Scumbag was known to be an arrogant man, who said whatever he felt, whenever he liked to anyone. He was a lanky, bandy-legged specimen, who wore his penny-loafers one or two sizes larger than he needed, strutting around the trading floor and dragging his feet under his carcass. He was well known for his shenanigans and even had the temerity to call a certain CTE reporter a nigger. He quickly apologized to the reporter after he was confronted by two black male brokers about his conduct. Mr. Scumbag's favorite mischief was to place a mirror on his shoe and then boldly place his foot between the legs of any unsuspecting female.

(4) Many could not forget a very pleasant Hispanic woman, who worked as a typist/clerk for a certain listed member-firm. She worked in a booth on the west-side of the trading floor and her duty was to type executed reports onto the member-system computers. Her apparent misfortune was that she was hearing impaired, and for no valid reason her persecutor who had more seniority, disliked her and often complained that she was too slow with her typing. It was an unfounded accusation since her volume of completed work often surpassed that of her miserable co-worker.

This beautiful hard-working individual was always well-dressed, polite to all around her; and was able to communicate effectively with everyone by lip-reading and speech. Many thought that it was pure jealousy on the part of her accuser. Her immediate Supervisor, who often plied between the CTE and the NYSE, never exercised his judgment to examine the validity of her accuser's claims, but decided to terminate her employment. She cried bitterly when she was told she had to go, she felt bewildered because she was the only breadwinner in the family.

(5) Another episode of injustice was the malicious teasing and torment of a young Asian woman, who was employed through the temp agency to work as a floor-runner for the Capital Trading Exchange. Her duties were to distribute written executed orders to the traders' booths. She was particularly taunted and ridiculed on the south side of the trading floor. Eventually, she mentally lost the capacity to deal with the daily ridicule and resorted to throwing cups of water down from the south balcony on to her persecutors. She was abruptly dismissed without a hearing, instead of being reprimanded and allowed to continue her employment in a different area of the trading-floor or in the tube-room which was located on the ground floor. Management was aware of the plight of this young woman all along, but did nothing to remedy the situation. On the CTE trading-floor, all brokers and their clerks had to be regarded as tin-gods. They were often rude and abusive to the CTE staff, and it was prohibited to reply in anyway.

EDWIN MANSFIELD—WHISTLEBLOWER

(a) One broker named Edwin Mansfield was a member of the Capital Trading Exchange from 1984 to 1990. He had quite a few complaints about trading activities, which were apparently credible, but he was met with stiff opposition and scolding. On April 26, 1999, a notable news organization published an article featuring the plaintiff Edwin Mansfield and some of the many allegations he made against the Board of Governors of the Capital Trading Exchange. After he was unceremoniously ousted from the exchange, he was treated with scorn, as though he had a bad disease and should be shunned. In fact some of the Brokers and Exchange Officials portrayed him as mentally imbalanced.

FEDERAL COURT
LOWER MANHATTAN
NEW YORK.

In a letter to the Federal District Court at 500 Pearl Street, New York, NY 10007, written by Mr. Edwin Mansfield and dated 9 December, 2001; quite a few of Mr. Edwin Mansfield's accusations were very serious indeed. The contents of that letter and others could not be revealed in this writing, since there was no apparent outcome; and the other accusations being very serious in nature and possibly libelous could not be independently corroborated by the author. Indeed, the contents of those letters were very scandalous and daring. This was a man who had everyone's welfare at heart, helping those he knew and did not know to obtain employment. He was a champion for justice, but when he became a whistle-blower he was let go from employment; the secret weapon used by those in authority to subvert his ability to fight his legal battles, and expose the illicit activities of the alleged violations.

THE INFORMANT OF THE CTE

❖ It also makes one wonder, if the Securities and Exchange Commission was ever aware of certain serious allegations by Mr. Mansfield on the whole; and if any action was taken. Here was a decent individual who claimed that he witnessed on a regular basis, the improprieties by power-brokers on the Capital Trading Exchange, and was trying to level the playing-field for traders and investors alike. Was he just naive or was he fearless of the consequences of exposing these illegal episodes?

❖ Officials of the Capital Trading Exchange were very stern in their warnings to all CTE employees on the trading-floor, never to write about nor divulge confidential information to the public. They were so serious, that printed forms were sent out to each trading floor employee demanding that they acknowledge and sign them, and return the said forms to the Human Resources Division. Intervention by the chairperson of the Floor Employees Union soon put a stop to that demand; and the forms became null and void. Furthermore, since the Capital Trading Exchange no longer exists as a separate viable entity, that directive is now null and void. What were they intending to hide from the public?

❖ Ten (10) excerpts about the Exchanges in New York were denied for reproduction by the rights-holder, after an arduous wait and the unsuccessful persistent attempts to gain permission on the author's behalf. Additionally, another several reproductions of other intellectual properties were denied by a second rights-holder.

❖ Thirteen (13) other juicier scandals of considerable substance could not be included in this book, because the rights-holders of two major newspapers, a major news organization, and a financial magazine did not deny permission to reprint the excerpts; but in fact demanded notorious prices as per article and a lot of administrative and legal hurdles that impeded the right to public knowledge. A sum total of twenty-three scandals had to be cut from this book, totaling approximately 37% of content.

❖ Those twenty-three (23) articles were originally published by the rights-holders for public reading, so why try to cover it all up now. If it was okay for public reading then, what has changed since then? The intended use of the excerpts, along with the personal interpolations of the author, was not in any way intended to be innocuous to any of the portrayed characters identified. The intention was simply to alert the investing public to the wiles of the Wall Street Executives.

❖ Notwithstanding the deletion of some major articles, the reader will still find enough to pique his or her interest. A wise investor should always seek to gain knowledge of the Stock Market through reading and research before investing.

REPORTERS ON THE CTE TRADING FLOOR

At the Capital Trading Exchange, many types of illegal activities were observed by Reporters, but Reporters were forbidden to intercede, comment, or make statements or to support Brokers in their complaints. The fact was that employees of the Trading Floor were not to police and or report observed illegal activities. That was not on their lists of duties and responsibilities. The more seasoned Reporters who worked in the most volatile and busy crowds were at times too busy to observe much of the illegal activities, especially since Reporters were cussed out and on rare occasions physically abused on a daily basis. Which reporter would give a damn about illegal trading activities, when they were just trying to survive and live to face another day of abuse?

POST SUPERVISORS ON THE CTE TRADING FLOOR

In the 1970's through the 1980's Reporters had to tolerate their Supervisors; of whom about 70 percent of them were square pegs in round holes. They had no formal training or grooming in a supervisory capacity and no GED or College credits to help their reasoning power. The junior trading floor staff was spoken to in very condescending tones as if they were children and doting imbeciles. Some of the junior staff were even better qualified than the Supervisors, and were both intellectually and more emotionally matured to cope with the job of supervising. Supervisors were not selected on merit but generally, the next supervisor was chosen from among the more senior of reporters in the "old boys and girls club". When it came to power—wow! Were they power drunk? Or was it because of the blatant use of drugs and alcohol? Those supervisors know who they were. Don't worry, there will be no insult added to injury by identifying any of you by name. What a classy bunch they were. Seventy percent of them drug users and alcoholics along with some of the most senior reporters working for the Capital Trading Exchange

Drug use by those supervisors and their senior reporter buddies were in plain sight on the street corners surrounding the Capital Trading Exchange, an overflow from the Trading Floor. Those disgusting events were so prevalent that undercover cops permeated the Capital Trading Exchange Trading Floor, and the surrounding street corners. Whenever there was a Transit Strike or a forecast of a really bad Snow-Storm, some trading floor staff was required to sleep over at the premises of the Capital Trading Exchange, in order that the next day's trading proceeded uninterrupted and adequately staffed. The celebrations began with an evening of alcohol and drugs and behavior unbecoming—it was even mentioned that there were sexual vulgarities performed by a female supervisor.

To assist supervisors in the performance of their duties, a Code of Conduct should have been established to train all staff to leave their personal problems at home, and their indifferences on the job outside the exchange, and further, to carry out their duties in a professional manner.

A review board would have been fine, to handle disputes and appeals concerning employee dismals and or improper conduct. The review board could have been expanded to deal with everyday disputes and complaints on the work site by trained and screened co-workers in labor/conflict dispute resolution, and to make impartial recommendations to management for final decision. Additionally, all member firm Specialists, Traders, and their Clerks should have been told; that making racial slurs and or insulting CTE Staff on the whole will not go unnoticed and unresolved. In the 1980's, racial bias and personal indifference abounded unmasked, and should not have been used by Post Supervisors to make critical decisions affecting who should be given recognition and incentive bonuses.

THE SUITS

Let's move unto one of "the suits—the big wig, the big fish, the SVP in charge of Trading Floor Operations" of whom there were a few, but only one can qualify as a douche-bag. What a disgusting, arrogant, insipid, and insidious, underhand bastard he was, who thought that he had the divine right to treat anyone and everyone in a cavalier manner and used these means to climb on the backs of others, and up the ladder of success. In other words, he behaved like the typical school yard bully. Perhaps he was abused as a child. A lot of unscrupulous deeds can be attributed to him, but should certain of his deeds be mentioned, he will be too easily identifiable. One deed for sure that rated him unconscionable, was when he often pulled a certain reporter from his duties on the floor whether the floor was busy or not; leaving others to take up the slack. The principal purpose being that, to discuss with that reporter the need for certain jobs to be done at his house. For example, that reporter did construction work or repairs, and the washing of the suit's car. This made that reporter feel untouchable from all other reporters and supervisors alike; he was free to take long lunch breaks or changed his break times as he so wished. Needless to say, that if you were the subject of complaint from that super reporter to the "suit"; you were black-listed.

Next, there was not only the use of drugs and alcohol by staff members during work hours, but on one occasion it seemed that practically 70% of all the Junior Management on the trading floor were involved in using CTE computers to entertain each other with vulgar e-mails. They were fortunate to keep their jobs with just a stern warning. Had there been a determination to harshly discipline one; the same action would have to be accorded to each and every one: thus causing chaos and disruption of the CTE's trading floor operations.

Some of the more senior Supervisors (old timers) were men of renown. Decent men with understanding respect for their sub-ordinates, who gave empathy and direction when and where it was needed.

RELIGIOUS LIBERTY AT THE CTE

Religious practices by Christians in particular before the day's trading or at lunch time got recognition and permission after persistent requests by junior staff. Not wanting to be left behind trailing in the dust kicked up by other companies, the CTE recognized the liberty of individuals to serve their God and conceded. This decision was more or less influenced by an article in a prominent news magazine. At that time, many large companies were hiring religious liberty style coordinators who came in any religious persuasion as requested by their staff. Contrary to what the CTE's upper echelon would have others believe, they were not in the forefront of religious tolerance in the workplace: behind the scenes it took some fight by some with strong religious fervor, to stand up for their right to worship and to witness on their break-times and before the start of the trading day. That was a particular victory for Christian believers, especially at a time when so many unbelievers are fighting to take "In God we Trust" and prayers out of the Courts, Schools and Congress.

BROKER/MEMBERS

A category of brokers known as Floor Officials were responsible for interpreting and making decisions on disputes between other brokers. If the brokers were dissatisfied with the decisions of the Floor Officials, they can go for a final decision from the "Senior Supervisory Officer" (a title used in the past) or the latter Floor Governor.

Brokers earn the privilege to trade for their own accounts or the accounts of others by purchasing or leasing a seat for a premium. The CTE was principally a Bond and Stock Market and eventually started trading in options (a derivative from the underlying stocks). Options trading started with just Call-Options and later around 1980 began trading both Call-Options and Put-Options. Eventually the Capital Trading Exchange became the second largest Options Exchange, after the "Chicago Board of Options Exchange."

As a result of Stocks and Derivatives along with Bonds being traded on the Capital Trading Exchange; there was established that there would be three types of Specialists namely:

1. The Options Specialist.   2. The Stock Specialist.   3. The Bond Specialist.

THE SPECIALIST RESPONSIBILITIES

An often asked question was: "What is the role or responsibility of the Specialist?" The reply was generally: "To maintain a fair and orderly market." Though true, there is much more to the answer than is readily expressed. Not to mention that a Broker / Specialist were required to be licensed, after studying for the Series 63 Exam. A synopsis of some of the other responsibilities is listed herein.

A designee so chosen by a listed company had the right and responsibility to register as a Specialist and to trade in one or more securities or its derivatives. The Specialist as a rule should avail him/herself or his senior clerk to be present on the floor of the Exchange by a specified time to process inquires. The Specialists bear the responsibilities for any and all orders or cancellations given to his/her clerks. Further at the close of the trading-day the Specialist or his/her clerk should remain on the floor for a period of time as designated and announced by the Stock Exchange.

A Specialist can on behalf of his/her specialist unit, apply to the Allocations Committee for a new listing of securities or its derivatives. This however, does not entitle him/her or their unit to be given the security on a first come first serve basis. The unit is considered for allocations after review, depending on filled out questionnaires and ratings of performance from traders; and the specialist unit's manpower and capital. Needless to state that in order for Specialists to gain favorable reviews from Trader/Brokers, certain unsavory favors were rendered to entice good reviews and allocation of an additional security.

The Specialist as a rule should never accept *discretionary orders* which could leave him open to ridicule and discipline. Notwithstanding this rule, it was common occurrence to see Specialists accepting such orders. In addition, the function of the Specialist in maintaining a fair and orderly market, allows him/her to trade for his/her own account. This account was permissible whenever there was a disparity between buy and sell orders in either full or odd-lot markets, and if it is reasonable and lacking in suspicion of an unorthodox guise, for the purpose of the maintenance of price and continuity, stability and fairness.

Among other things, triple listing or quadruple listing of Options (a derivative of stocks) became a real sore point for Specialists and a burdensome catastrophe for the Trading Analysis Department. This was so because of the ridiculous quoting systems of some Exchanges where Bids were sometimes higher than offers (e.g. 2 1/4 Bids to 2 1/16 Offers) hence parameters that were too high, some exchange systems that were not updating, and some Exchanges trading through each other's prices. Of course this was prior to the Exchanges Operating Systems which were modernized and automated.

Who's monitoring these screens on a daily basis for irregularities, and who would have the right answers for the investing public and listed companies? Trading Analysis did not have all the tools for monitoring and the proximity to the Specialists and Brokers to make all the right trading decisions. The hope and implementation to a large degree that "Service Desk Coordinators" and the "System Support Staff" can reconcile most of the problems before Trading Analysis Department is inundated with complaints.

TRADING OPTIONS

The characteristics of standardized options are many and complex. An option contract is defined as a Put or Call Option which are derivatives of their underlining securities that carry a unit of trade, strike price and expiration date. All options of the same derivative and strike price and expiration date are referred to as being an option series. There is no need to get into all aspects of the characteristics, strategies and risks of trading options. Leave that for those who are seeking to establish a career in Stock Market Brokerage, perhaps as an "Option Principal Member (OPM) which entails intense study and the purchase or lease of and OPM seat.

For instance, if one wanted to study to be an Option Principal Member (OPM), they can purchase a book on how to become an options trader. Studying for the SERIES-7examination is very demanding, covering many chapters, and hundreds of pages. Some books even include a CD-ROM as a study-aid and practice exams. Other exams include the series 6 for mutual funds traders and the series 63 for registered stock brokers.

A Stock Option is a contract giving the owner the right to buy or sell shares or units of the underlying security at a specific price and expiration date. As an option buyer the most you can lose is the price you paid for the option.

THE FEEL GOOD MOTTO

During the Hay-days of the Capital Trading Exchange auction market, just before a hectic opening of a large block-sale of stock or an eventual opening of its derivatives confusion abounded. Floor-brokers who were poised like Cobras to strike on the best bids and offers uneasily jostled for a good vantage point in the crowd which lent itself to an aura of mild hostility and shouting; and lewd comments. Both exchange employees and brokers got their tongue lashings.

As the regular or delayed opening is declared ready for trading, one can sometimes hear the Specialist say—"lets rock and roll", and trading starts. There have been times when a broker for one medical reason or other may have fallen to the floor, whether semi-conscious or otherwise. Does trading in that crowd stop? No!—on the contrary his fellow brokers walk around or step over the fallen in order to take advantage of trade opportunities. It was usually up to the CTE staff to promptly call the medical department for a Doctor and an Exchange Security Officer.

The object on every brokers mind was to consummate their trades and make some money for their accounts or their brokerage houses at any cost. Being ill does not preclude a broker reporting to work. Make that money at any cost. Hence the traders motto—"It's better to look good than to feel good".

THE CAPITAL TRADING EXCHANGE OPERATING SYSTEM

Here is a glimpse of The Capital Trading Exchange floor operations system, using acronyms and explaining their meanings to give the layperson an elementary understanding of the day to day operations of the typical Stock Exchange in the United States. Even before the trading day began The Capital Trading Exchange staff, namely Managers, Supervisors, Reporters and Coordinators; reported to work early in the mornings to ensure that all systems were up and running.

CCRS: CTE Card Reader System—A trading floor area network which read data from marked-sensed card readers and displays it to the other operational and display screens. This was phased out about two decades ago, when the system became more technologically advanced.

CDS: CTE Display System—Displays on overhead monitors showing Bids, offers, last sale prices and volumes for CTE Equities, Bonds and Options.

COF / GTC: CTE Order File / Good till Cancelled Order—An enhancement to the card reading system to allow retention from day to day of GTC orders which came through the system but were not executed. This was implemented in early 1988, and gradually phased out.

COTS: CTE Option Trading System—A system developed by an electronic company called Quotron, which displayed on overhead screens/monitors, option bids, offers and last sale prices and volume.

AUTOCLEAR: A service which generated date for submission into clearance for orders executed. In the olden days member firms and their back office staff used to work early in the mornings and late at nights to resolve trading errors and matches. That came to an end when trades were matched electronically.

AUTOEX: A selective service which automatically executed market and executable limit orders of up to ten contracts against the current quoted market. The service was also designed to protect orders on the Specialists books with a guarantee of a single price. Trade executions were reported back via computers to the public, giving immediate execution reports.

AUTOPER /AUTOAMOS: An automated messaging system which was introduced in 1979, that routed orders to touch sensitive screens for execution by the Specialist. This system gave timely executions, decreased the use of written tickets, eliminated clerical errors and cut down considerably the paper trash on the trading floor.

BRIDGE / QUOTE / OPO: A theoretical Options Pricing System developed to calculated option prices and send those prices to multiple overhead display screens.

CMS: Common Message Switch which automatically routed orders and messages from member firms to the Exchange floors and the relative trading posts. It also sent messages of Buy/Sell orders and execution reports back to the respective firms.

CQS: Consolidated Quote System—which electronically reported all equity quotations to Market Data Vendors.

CTA: Consolidated Tape Association—which is a network of all equity marketplaces which administers and makes polices for the consolidated tape network.

CTS: Consolidated Trade System—This reported all equity trades to market Data Vendors.

DSR: Direct Sale Reporting—allowed sales to be electronically reported directly to "the tape".

EE / EG: Electronic Entry and Electronic Gateway—these terms were synonymous, and was a central collector of data from the trading floor which processed the information to various systems.

QQ: Quick Quote update reporting from a touch sensitive screen used by reporters.

QUOTE / TRADE: These touch screen EE devices were used by reporters during and after the "marked-sensed" cards were phased out.

ETHERNET: A standard method of communicating among various users of a common network.

LAN: Local Area Networks—LANs were cables over which information is transported, and can be thought of as telephone party lines where many devices share one cable.

CMDS: CTE Market Data System—Computers that received trades and quotes from the floor, validate symbol and price, log them for future use, and send them to "the tape".

COARS: CTE Opening Automated Report System—A selective service system which facilitated the opening of options and equity issues. The system matches buy, sell, and market orders and reports executions back to the entering firms based on an opening price entered by the Specialist. Notwithstanding the hectic opening of the day's trades, investors can rest assured of accurate reports on their option and equity orders. Thanks to upgraded technology.

COPRA: CTE Options Price Reporting Authority—Like the consolidated tape association, this is an association of options marketplaces which administered and managed the COPRA high speed vendor line. This line sent option trades and quotes to market data vendors.

CPCS: Price collector System—A computer which is part of the CTE operational system. It got its prices from other marketplaces such as the "Toronto Stock Exchange" and send the prices to the CTE overhead display monitors.

CTE PER / AMOS: Post Execution Reporting / Amex Options Switch—one of the oldest operating system introduced in 1979. These systems received small orders from CMS and route them to the appropriate post. After execution of the orders, the reports were sent out by mark-sensed cards via in-post electronic card readers. Later, coordinators were placed at the service desk to monitor order executions, answer queries form the Brokers and their clerks; and help to resolve trading execution errors.

CTE QUICK QUOTE: This system was introduced in 1984, facilitating Option and Equity Quote updates from touch sensitive screens which were used by Post Reporters. This was a technological advance from the old system of mark-sensed cards which were prone to smudging, errors and delays of executed trades; especially because of the malfunction of the conveyor-belt system that was use on each post that often malfunctioned.

CTE QUICK TRADE: The reporting of actual trades using the same touch screen systems manned by reporters, that made the execution and reporting of sales speedier.

CTE RAPID QUOTE: The ability to target multiple option strike prices at the same time for speedy updates to the public, for both options and equities. This was done by Reporters using EE devices / touch screens, located on the outer perimeters of the trading posts.

CTE SEB: Specialist Electronic Book—An electronic system used by the specialists and their clerks to execute limited orders automatically.

CTE SUSM: Special Underlying Securities Monitor—A system developed that displayed equity bids, offers last sale prices and the volumes for equities, using overhead display screens that gave speedy information to traders.

CTE TOPS /XTOPS: These two electronic display books were introduced in 1989 for the use by Specialists, for pricing of options. These systems automatically calculated new quotes for an entire options class based on the changes in the value of the underlying security or index.

Some of the explanations of the provided acronyms were simplified in order for the layperson to better understand how the Stock Market worked. New electronic technology, whilst being immensely beneficial to both the Stock Exchange and the investing public; it has eliminated the need for the "Two Dollar Brokers' executing trades on commission and cut dramatically the need for floor-runners.

Chapter Two

AGENCIES THAT INFLUENCE THE STOCK MARKETS

THE SECURITIES AND EXCHANGE COMMISSION

(1) Investors and the general public have always been intrigued and fascinated by the work of the Securities and Exchange Commission (SEC), but admittedly not very knowledgeable about its structure and function. It was imperative, that the general public should be well informed of the formation and function of the SEC; if they were to fully understand why their involvement in the Stock Markets, with trading violations, were there to protect the public, and maintain a fair, orderly and legal system. The Securities and Exchange Commission was established to oversee all Self-Regulatory Organizations (SRO). This was prompted by the precipitous drop in stock prices from 1929 to the year 1933. To clearly define the SEC and its functions, this synopsis is provided.

SEC Formation:

(a) According to Susan P. Shapiro, "The Securities and Exchange Commission (SEC) of course, is the preeminent protector of the capital markets in this country. A New Deal agency, the SEC was born in 1934 in the aftermath of the great stock crash and the revelation that abusive corporate financial and trading practices, which contributed to the debacle, were endemic. It is an independent regulatory agency, headed by five commissioners, with broad responsibility for the regulation of publically held corporations, the securities markets, and the professionals who serve them. Federal securities legislation requires that companies wishing to offer securities for public sale first file with the SEC a registration statement disclosing business and financial information and that they subsequently provide continuing and updated disclosure through annual and other periodic reports, proxy materials, and the like. The SEC processes these disclosure materials and serves as an informational conduit to investors. It does not, however, rule on or guarantee the soundness of securities offered. The agency also regulates broker-dealers, investment advisors, investment companies, public utility holding companies, stock exchanges, and national securities associations, and it plays an advisory role in the bankruptcy reorganization proceedings of publically held companies. Agency staff has the responsibility for the enforcement of the federal securities laws and the control of fraud and have authority to conduct inspections and investigations and institute civil and administrative proceedings. These responsibilities are carried out by the SEC headquarters office in Washington and regional and branch offices in fifteen cities. The SEC is a relatively small agency as federal agencies go, with roughly two thousand employees nationwide (the Internal Revenue Service has thirty-four times as many employees) and a budget representing only about .01 percent of the annual federal budget in recent years." (Shapiro, Wayward Capitalists, 1984), 4-5

SEC Investigative Work

(b) Susan Shapiro expresses that, "Federal securities statutes authorize the SEC to conduct investigations to determine whether these laws have been violated. In most cases, investigations are private and the materials gathered confidential to ensure the cooperation of witnesses and to protect persons about whom unfounded or unsubstantiated charges have been made . . . . Surprisingly little is known about the conduct of SEC investigations. The SEC is a low-profile agency. Its annual reports and assorted publications reveal little about the organization and of its work. The agency has had few scandals and the attendant journalistic and congressional scrutiny that follow in their wake. Its current and former employees have been sufficiently loyal or insufficiently literary or entrepreneurial to generate the expose's common in other regulatory agency settings. (136) . . . Investigations are conducted by the Division of Enforcement in SEC headquarters as well as by nine regional offices located in New York, Boston, Washington, Atlanta, Chicago, Fort Worth, Denver, Los Angeles, and Seattle and by six branch offices. With over two hundred staffers (about 11 percent of all SEC personnel), the New York regional office is by far the largest. Six percent of all agency staff works in the Chicago regional office, 5 percent in Los Angeles, 4 percent in Washington, and 2-3 percent in the other regional offices. (137) . . . 'The primary responsibility for investigation rests with the Commission's regional administrators whose investigators conduct most of the field work' (Annual Report 1951, 154). Prior to the 1960s enforcement activities conducted by the regional offices were supervised and coordinated by a skeleton staff in the headquarters Division of Trading and Exchanges (which also had responsibility for the regulation of broker-dealers, supervision of exchanges and other self-regulatory agencies, and market surveillance." (Shapiro, Wayward Capitalists, 1984), 138

SEC Detection to Prosecution

(c) Susan Shapiro continues, "Civil actions are initiated by SEC staff in the federal district courts. Typically, they are injunctive proceedings, the successful outcome of which enjoins offenders from future violations of the securities laws. In some instances, other forms of ancillary relief may be secured, for example, the appointment of receivers or supplemental investigation or disclosure. Injunctions are imposed where violations are ongoing or have a high likelihood of reoccurrence. Through temporary restraining orders and preliminary and permanent injunctions, civil actions seek to halt illegal activities. In an emergency, a temporary restraining order can be obtained in a matter of hours, thereby freezing corporate assets before they are pilfered. Although contested proceedings may involve protracted litigation, injunctive actions frequently are resolved by consent, in which offenders neither admit nor deny any wrongdoing, [As you will see later in upcoming excerpts of illicit activities by traders and executives alike] but agree they will not violate the securities laws in the future. Failure to abide by an injunctive decree can result in criminal contempt proceedings. There is no other sanction attached to the injunction, although it may serve as a bar from future activities in the securities industry or as the basis for revocation of registration with the SEC. There are no restrictions on the characteristics of the parties subject to civil remedies. They may be individuals or organizations, securities issuers, professionals, or ordinary citizens. The administrative proceeding is a private or public hearing, ordered by the commission, and presided over by an SEC administrative law judge. Some are lengthy and complex, with the presentation of numerous documents and witnesses; others are settled by consent or default without formal hearings. Administrative law judges recommend a disposition to the SEC commissioners, who render the final disposition in the case. Respondents can request oral argument before the commission and can appeal its decision to the federal courts. Although the law concerning the utilization of the SEC administrative proceeding has changed somewhat over the years, it is generally available for persons or organizations bearing some kind of relationship to the SEC, either as registrants or their employees or as professionals who practice before the agency (that is, attorneys or accountants). The most severe sanction in an administrative proceeding terminates this relationship—the registration of a broker-dealer or investment advisor is revoked or the professional is barred from practice before the commission. Less radical sanctions and ancillary remedies associated with administrative proceedings include temporary suspensions of business, employment, association with a regulated firm, or trading; expulsion or suspension from self—regulatory organizations; censure; alterations in the management or supervisory structure of the organization; restrictions on business practices; and the voluntary withdrawal of the party from the securities business. (153) At last the role and function of the SEC becomes clear. It is the symbolic guarantor of trust in securities. The creation of the SEC was a clever innovation. It allowed government to fabricate and guarantee the trust that the securities markets had lost. But the agency's initial promises of trust were only provisional; ultimately the SEC had to earn the trust of securities investors by deed rather than by word. So far the agency has performed well. Where other regulatory agencies have consistently earned the mockery and distress of the American public, the reputation of the SEC has remained relatively untarnished and its role as symbolic guarantor of trust in the securities markets unquestioned. (Cary 1964, 661; Ratner 1978, 2-3; Miller 1979b, DI; Subcommittee 1976, 11; Karmel 1982).

But shoring up the shaky foundation of trust is a lifetime job. With the slightest inattention or temporary lethargy, the capitalist structure might easily come crashing down. And this is where detection comes in. Obviously, the SEC cannot eliminate securities fraud. It is not necessary that it do so. But to maintain trust, the agency must reduce the opportunities for law breaking and insure complete enforcement coverage and the guarantee that no person, no corporation, no scheme is inherently immune from the enforcement process. Investors must believe that all wayward capitalists with whom they may inadvertently become involved have a real chance (<u>and</u> ideally a good one) of being caught by SEC enforcers and their illicit activities halted. Trust is therefore premised on universalistic application of the enforcement process.

Coverage or selective immunity or vulnerability to enforcement is a byproduct of detention. The orchestration of detection strategies determines which wayward capitalists will be caught and which will be allowed to freely ply their trade, the likelihood that certain kinds of violators will be snared or spared, the likelihood that certain kinds of investors will be protected or victimized, and the likelihood that acts of wayward capitalism will be nipped in the bud or allowed to grow and flourish without disruption. SEC enforcers can easily maintain a respectable-size investigative caseload with little effort, imagination, or vigilance. And in this era of government contraction, budget cutting, and deregulation, the temptation certainly is to do just that. But the integrity of trust requires coverage as well as numbers. It requires that the full arsenal of investigative strategies be refined and deployed so that all forms of wayward capitalism are vulnerable to SEC enforcement. If word of selective enforcement leaked out, if securities fraud scandals became a common feature of the capitalist landscape, the shaky foundation of trust might crumble and the investment monies that feed the capitalist beast dry up." (Sus841), 190-191

THE FEDERAL RESERVE

(2) Wikipedia Encyclopedia reports that, "The Federal Reserve System (also known as the Federal Reserve, and informally as the Fed) is the central banking system of the United States. It was created on December 23, 1913 with the enactment of the Federal Reserve Act, largely in response to a series of financial panics, particularly a severe panic in 1907. Over time, the roles and responsibilities of the Federal Reserve System have expanded and its structure has evolved. Events such as the Great Depression were major factors leading to changes in the system. The Congress established three key objectives for monetary policy—maximum employment, stable prices, and moderate long-term interest rates—in the Federal Reserve Act. The first two objectives are sometimes referred to as the Federal Reserve's dual mandate. Its duties have expanded over the years and today, according to official Federal Reserve documentation, include conducting the nation's monetary policy, supervising and regulating banking institutions, maintaining the stability of the financial system and providing financial services to depository institutions, the U.S. government, and foreign official institutions.

NEW YORK FEDERAL RESERVE

The Fed also conducts research into the economy and releases numerous publications such as the Beige Book. The Federal Reserve System's structure is composed of the presidentially appointed Board of Governors (or Federal Reserve Board), the Federal Open Market Committee (FOMC), twelve regional Federal Reserve Banks located in major cities throughout the nation, numerous privately owned U.S. member banks and various advisory councils. The FOMC is the committee responsible for setting monetary policy and consists of all seven members of the Board of Governors and the twelve regional bank presidents, though only five bank presidents vote at any given time. The Federal Reserve System has both private and public components, and was designed to serve the interests of both the general public and private bankers. The result is a structure that is considered unique among central banks. It is also unusual that an entity outside the central bank, namely the United States Department of the Treasury, creates the currency used. According to the Board of Governors, the Federal Reserve is independent within government in that 'its monetary policy decisions do not have to be approved by the President or anyone else in the executive or legislative branches of government.' Its authority is derived from statutes enacted by the U.S. Congress and the System is subject to congressional oversight. The members of the Board of

Governors, including its chairman and vice-chairman, are chosen by the President and confirmed by the Senate. The government also exercises some control over the Federal Reserve by appointing and setting the salaries of the system's highest-level employees. Thus the Federal Reserve has both private and public aspects. The U.S. Government receives all of the system's annual profits, after a statutory dividend of 6% on member banks' capital investment is paid, and an account surplus is maintained. In 2010, the Federal Reserve made a profit of $82 billion and transferred $79 billion to the U.S. Treasury. This was followed at the end of 2011 with a transfer of $77 billion in profits to the U.S. Treasury Department." (Wikipedia, Federal Reserve System)

CONGRESSIONAL ACTIONS—NCFRR

Wikipedia Encyclopedia states, "The National Commission on Fiscal Responsibility and Reform (often called Bowles-Simpson/Simpson-Bowles from the names of co-chairs Alan Simpson and Erskine Bowles; or NCFRR) IS A Presidential Commission created in 2010 by President Barack Obama to identify " . . . policies to improve the fiscal situation in the medium term to achieve fiscal sustainability over the long run." The commission first met on April 27, 2010. A report was released on December1, 2010, but failed a vote on December3, with 11 of 18 votes in favor, with a supermajority of 14 votes needed to formally endorse the blueprint. Critics say that it would cut entitlement and safety net programs, including Social Security and Medicare.

The original proposal for a commission came from bipartisan legislation that would have required Congress to vote on its recommendations as presented, without any amendment. In January 2010, that bill failed in the Senate by a vote of 53—46, when six Republicans who had co-sponsored it nevertheless voted against it. Thereafter, Obama established the Commission by Executive Order 13531. Former Republican Senator Alan Simpson (R-Wyo) after his appointment to co-chair the Commission criticized the former supporters who had voted against the bill, saying that their purpose "was to stick it to the President." In the absence of special legislation, the Commission's proposals are not guaranteed to be considered by Congress in a single up-or-down vote.

The Commission includes 18 members and one executive director appointed by the President. They include six members of the U.S. House of Representatives, and six members of the U.S. Senate. The first vote on the final recommendations, originally set for December 1, 2010, was detailed until December 3, when the commission fell short of the supermajority of 14 of 18 votes needed to approve the report. The eleven voting for it were six Democrats

(Bowles, Conrad, Durbin, Fudge, Rivlin, and Spratt) and five Republicans (Coburn, Cote, Crapo, Gregg, Simpson); the seven voting against it were four Democrats (Baucas, Becerra, Schakowsky, Stern) and three Republicans (Camp, Hensarling, Ryan).

On November 10, NCFRR co-chairs Simpson and Bowles released a draft proposal for consideration by other commission members. The proposal presented five 'steps'

(a) $200 billion reduction per year in discretionary spending with proposed cuts including reducing defense procurement by 15% and closing one third of overseas bases, eliminating earmarks, and cutting the Federal work-force by 10%.
(b) $100 billion in increased tax revenues through various tax reform proposals, such as introducing a 15 cent per gallon gasoline tax and eliminating or restricting a variety of tax deductions such as the home mortgage interest deduction and the deduction for employer-provided healthcare benefits.
(c) Controlling health care costs by maintaining the Medicare cost controls associated with the recent health care reform legislation, in addition to considering a public option and a further increase in the authority of Independent Payment Advisory Board.
(d) A reduction in entitlements, including farm subsidies, civilian and military federal pensions and student loan subsidies.
(e) Modifications to the Social Security program to raise the payroll tax and the retirement age.

[The Healthcare Reform Bill proposed by President Barack Obama, (also known as Obama-care) met with total impasse by members of the Republican Party. Rage was expressed across the country principally by Republican supporters; and Presidential candidate Mitt Romney swore that he will repeal "Obama-care" on the first day of his Presidency. However, Mitt Romney in his quest for the White House and the opportunity to discredit and oppose much of President Obama's proposals; failed to win the national elections.]

. . . Criticism—The commission has been criticized as deliberating in secret and as being 'stacked with the people who want to target entitlement spending rather than any balanced proposal. Because it could lead to cuts in benefits for Social Security and Medicare, many Democrats are calling this a "cat food" commission, meaning that it will eliminate key portions of the social safety net, forcing the poor and elderly into such poverty that they will only be able to afford cat food.

Liberal and senior's organizations have criticized the inclusion of several staffers who are paid by private groups, such as the Peter G. Peterson Foundation and Committee for a responsible Federal Budget, who have previously advocated cuts to entitlement programs, although the panel said that other staffers are paid by liberal groups such as the Economic Policy Institute.

Keynesian Economist James K. Galbraith submitted a statement to the NCFRR on behalf of Americans for Democratic Action. He argued that the current deficits were caused by the financial crisis; that cuts in Social Security and Medicare would be harmful and would not reduce the deficit; and that the Commission would do best 'by advancing no proposals at all.'

Dean Baker of the Center for Economic and Policy Research in Washington criticizes the deficit report for omitting a tax on the financial industry, as was recommended by the International Monetary Fund. He also denounces co-chairs Alan K. Simpson and Erskine Bowles for claiming to have looked everywhere on ways to increase revenue, but not including the financial industry. Also Baker said that a possible conflict of interest exists regarding Erskine Bowles for serving on the board of Morgan Stanley while being on the commission and asks for further investigation into the connection between Bowles' role as a director of Morgan Stanley and the omission of any financial taxes in the report.

Krugman wrote, Simpson-Bowles is terrible. It mucks around with taxes but is obsessed with lowering marginal rates despite a complete absence of evidence that is important. It offers nothing on Medicare that isn't in the Affordable Care Act. And it raises the Social Security retirement age because lie expectancy has risen—completely ignoring the fact that life expectancy has only gone up for the well-off and well-educated, while stagnating or even declining among the people who need the program most." (Wikipedia, National Commission on Fiscal Responsibility and Reform, 2012)

DODD—FRANK WALL STREET REFORM

> Wikipedia Encyclopedia expresses that, "The Dodd—Frank Wall Street Reform and Consumer Protection Act was signed into federal law by Present Barack Obama on July 21, 2010. Passed as a response to the late 2000s recession, it brought the most significant changes to financial regulation in the United States since the regulatory reform that followed the great depression. It made changes in the American financial regulatory environment that affect all federal financial regulatory agencies and almost every part of the nation's financial services industry.

As with other major financial reforms, a variety of critics have attacked the law, some arguing that it was not enough to prevent another financial crisis or more 'bail-outs', and others arguing it went too far and unduly restricted financial institutions. [November 7, 2012, the day after the American Elections, the proclamation was that President Barack Obama was re-elected to a second term—and the Dow Jones dropped more than 200 points. Wall Street disliked the fact that there was a victory for Pres. Barack Obama because of this Reform Act—it impeded their ability to continue business as usual. However, it was a victory for the 99%. Wall Street executives preferred a victory for Mitt Romney who would have repealed the Dodd—Frank Reform Act. Additionally, it was said that the drop on the Dow Jones was impacted by the European Central Bank and the Global economic crisis. However, the election victory was a defeat for hate, disrespect, derision, racial bias and partisan politics.] The law was initially proposed by the Obama Administration in June 2009, when the White House sent a series of proposed bills to Congress. A version of the legislation was introduced in the House in July 2009. On December 2, 2009, revised versions were introduced in the House of Representatives by Financial Services Committee Chairman Barney Frank and in the Senate Banking Committee by Chairman Chris Dodd. Due to their involvement with the bill, the conference committee that reported on June 25, 2010, voted to name the bill after the two members of Congress .... The financial Crisis of 2007—2010, led to widespread calls for changes in the regulatory system. In June 2009, President Obama introduced a proposal for a 'sweeping overhaul of the United States financial regulatory system, a transformation on a scale not seen since the reforms that followed the Great Depression.

As the financial bill emerged from conference, President Obama stated that the bill included 90% of the proposals. Major components of Obama's original proposal, listed by order in which they appear in the 'A New Foundation' outline, include

(i) The consolidation of regulatory agencies, elimination of the national thrift charter, and new oversight council to evaluate systemic risk,
(ii) Comprehensive regulation of financial markets, including increased transparency of derivatives (bringing them onto exchanges);
(iii) Consumer protection reforms including a new consumer protection agency and uniform standards for 'plain vanilla' products as well as strengthened investor protection;

(iv) Tools for financial crises, including a 'resolution regime' complimenting the existing Federal Deposit Insurance Corporation (FDIC) authority to allow for orderly winding down of bankrupt firms, and including a proposal that the Federal Reserve (the 'Fed') receive authorization from the Treasury for extensions of credit in 'unusual and exigent circumstances';
(v) Various measures aimed at increasing international standards and cooperation including proposals related to improved accounting and tightened regulation of credit rating agencies." (Wikipedia, Dodd—Frank Wall Street Reform and Consumer Protection Act, 2012)

Chapter Three

HOLDING ACCOUNTANTS ACCOUNTABLE

A lot of Ponzi schemes, collapses, and bankruptcy filings could have been avoided if Congress had heeded Representative Wyden's proposal, and not sided with the big money lobbyists.

(1) Reporter Larry Reynolds writes, 'Forty percent of the savings and loan failures were caused by fraud and abuse by insiders, claims Rep. Ron Wyden (D-Ore.), who is leading a drive in Congress to 'toughen up' reporting and accounting procedures for all companies. 'Each of these institutions had in-house accountants charged with implementing responsible internal controls for the S&L. Each institution had outside accountants charged with making independent assessments of the institution's books to ensure the financial statements correctly reflected the condition of the S&L. These accountants were supposed to be the nation's first line of defense against fraud. Clearly, these defenses failed,' Wyden says. While outraged by the magnitude and cost of the financial fraud found in the S&L industry, which is now expected to cost American taxpayers $500 billion, Wyden feels the debacle only reflects a basic flaw in the current overall business regulatory and accounting system. 'Our financial reporting system doesn't require accountants to directly inform regulators when their clients engage in fraud or other illegalities. The current system is a

loophole-ridden morass that consists of little more than accountants telling management when they've uncovered fraud at their company. It does virtually nothing to protect the public from the kinds of rip offs by sleazy operators that took place with the S&L's,' Wyden explains. His answer to this situation is to make all SEC-regulated companies issue a report on their internal management controls, and then require that their auditors publicly evaluate this study. Besides verifying the books, Wyden and the General Accounting Office feel that outside accounting firms should be required to search for any possible illegal acts committed by the company executives during their audits and report them directly to the SEC. The current practice requires auditors to simply resign the account and notify the SEC they're no longer working for that company. Wyden's proposal worries the business community and has resulted in a flurry of activity aimed at defeating the legislation, which seem to be gaining ground in Congress. [There is Congress at work, not doing the work of the people. Congress is perpetual about seeking their personal gains and interests, not only in this new era, but in decades gone by.] Industry groups are afraid that the current anti-fraud atmosphere may lead to legislation fundamentally changing the traditional confidential accountant-client relationship into one where outside private auditors are transformed into corporate cops . . . . 'This legislation was introduced in response to the S&L crisis. However, it does not target the offenders, but instead imposes increased regulation and cost on all public companies which are already required by law to have adequate internal controls,' Roy argues. 'This bill could turn all accountants into government policemen,' notes Washington corporate lobbyist Jim Kaitz. 'If an outside auditor has a concern, it should be able to sit down with its client and discuss the problem with them rather than being forced to run to the SEC.' Kaitz and other business advocates also argue that current SEC requirements already are strong enough to correct any problems and protect the investing public. 'There is no clear public benefit as this only duplicates existing SEC regulations and proposals. Congress should not leapfrog the process and preempt the orderly regulatory actions of the SEC,' Roy Maintains. [That decision was obviously a big blunder by Congress, going on the misguided premise that; the then regulatory rules were enough to protect the investing public.] According to industry estimates, about one of four public companies already publish some sort of public report on their internal controls—the number jumps to 60 percent for Fortune 500firms. If passed, the Wyden bill would increase overall audit fees by 5 percent for companies with good external control systems, and up to 20 percent for others. 'It's just another way for accountants to generate more business and fatten their fees in a very competitive market,' comments John Jacobs of Political Profiles, a Washington public affairs consulting firm. Moreover, companies would have to create another layer of 'paper defenses' to justify their actions as protection from their own auditors. 'The fee increase is real, but small change for most of these SEC firms,' argues a House Committee Staffer. 'Besides, business is just making our argument when they say 25 percent of publicly traded companies already have some kind of internal report card. To us, that means 75 percent don't. And that's the woodpile where most of the crooks are likely to be hiding.' By last fall, the Big Six accounting firms were already facing over 20 government suits and a possible $1.5 billion in damages for alleged misconduct connected with the collapse of various S&L associations. This has created both a public relations and financial nightmare for auditors. In turn, it has generated a concern in the corporate sector that if the Wyden bill passed, accountants would err on the side of super caution—running to the SEC with any small details they discovered while auditing a client's books—in an effort to improve their public image and protect themselves from government investigations. 'No company wants to be tainted with the image of having a poor internal control system, or maybe having done something illegal. Just the whisper of the possibility of something like that could drive down its stock and create all kinds of problems with investors, bankers, suppliers, joint venture partners—you name it,' notes a senior financial officer at a Fortune 100 firm. 'To have your accountant turn you over to the SEC because there *may* be a problem would be like being judged in the press before the SEC even decided a trial was necessary.' In response, business groups are taking financial fraud and 'beefing up' management internal control reports more seriously. For instance, over the past several years, the Treadway Commission, a panel supported by private business and the financial industry, has been studying this issue. Last March, the commission issued a paper on the best ways to institute these controls for companies that don't currently have them, while giving others a state-of-the-art blueprint for refining their present systems. Besides its educational value, the report was part of a deal cut between industry and Wyden, who promised not to push his bill until business could respond with a solution of its own. 'The report was a nice review of the accounting literature and presented a very good *cookbook* for those executives who want to install a reporting control system in their company,' notes a senior Wyden aide. 'But it didn't justify sitting on our hands while we gave them time to respond to our concerns.' Looking to cut a deal of its own, the American Institute of Certified Public Accounts (AICPA) and a separate low profile working group comprising the major national accounting firms have promised Wyden they will support a limited version of his legislation. The accountants agreed to back a bill which mandates that management must file a public report on its internal control, which will be evaluated by its auditors. However, these reports will only relate to the financial statement preparation process for SEC-regulated corporations. In other words accountants will not report on any other improprieties or illegalities that don't directly pertain to the company's financial statement. Also auditors will only report possible fraud or wrong doing to the SEC after first giving a company's senior managers and board of directors an opportunity to review, comment and correct the problem. The accounting community also has agreed to support legislation requiring that banks, S&Ls and other financial institutions report their audit findings to the SEC rather than just to the federal banking regulators. The Kicker!? 'As long as they act in good faith,' accountants can't be sued for libel for five years after the bill is passed, if clients they turn over to the SEC are later found innocent of any misconduct. [This allows for major cover-ups by big companies misusing investors' funds. What was with the AICPA? Were they shaking in their boots for fear of being sued, instead of being willing to use their professional skills thereby protecting the public and reducing the chances of Savings and Loans collapses? They could have opted or rather demanded legislation for immunity from prosecution by Banks, S&Ls, and other Financial Institutions.] 'We felt we had only two choices: Let Wyden go ahead with his original bill, which could be risky in this Congress, or work with him to get something we thought was do-able,' says Joe Moragilo of the AICPA. 'I understand that the accountants felt they had to respond to the political pressures on them. But I feel they did it at the expense of their clients,' says lobbyist Kaitz. 'But, let's be clear about something. This was a compromise between Wyden and the accounting community, not between Congress and the business lobby. As far as we are concerned, this is still a terrible bill and we are going to defeat it." (Reynolds, 1991)

AUTOMOTIVE INDUSTRY CRISIS OF 2008-2010

(2) Wikipedia Encyclopedia reports, "The automotive industry crisis of 2008-2010 was a part of a global financial downturn. The crisis affected European and Asian automobile manufacturers, but it was primarily felt in the American automobile manufacturing industry. The downturn also affected Canada by virtue of the Automotive Products Trade Agreement. The automotive industry was weakened by a substantial increase in the prices of automotive fuels linked to the 2003-2008 energy crisis which discouraged purchases of sport utility vehicles (SUVs) and pickup trucks which have low fuel economy. The popularity and the relatively high profit margins of these vehicles had encouraged the American 'Big Three' automakers, General Motors, Ford, and Chrysler to make them their primary focus. With fewer fuel-efficient models to offer to consumers, sales began to slide. By 2008, the situation had turned critical as the credit crunch placed pressure on the prices of raw materials. Car companies from Asia, Europe, North America, and elsewhere have implemented creative marketing strategies to entice reluctant consumers as most experienced double-digit percentage declines in sales. Major manufacturers, including the "Big Three" and Toyota offered substantial discounts across their lineups. The Big Three faced criticism for their lineups, which were seen to be irresponsible in light of rising fuel prices. North American consumers turned to the smaller, cheaper, more fuel efficient imports from Japan and Europe. However, many of the vehicles perceived to be foreign were actually 'transplants' foreign cars manufactured or assembled in the United States, at lower cost than the imports . . . . The Canadian auto industry is closely linked to the U.S., due to the Automotive Products Trade Agreement and later the North American Free Trade Agreement (NAFTA) and is in similar trouble . . . . The crisis of the United States is mainly defined by the government rescue of both General Motors and Chrysler. Ford secured a line of credit in case they required a bridging loan in the near future. Car sales declined in the United States, affecting both U.S. based and foreign car manufacturers. The bridging loan led to greater scrutiny of the U.S. automotive industry in addition to criticism of their product range, product quality, high labor wages, and job bank programs. The government backed rescue of the American auto industry gained the support of 50% of Americans in 2012 according to a Pew Research Center poll. While the "Big Three" U.S. market share declined from 70% in 1998 to 53% in 2008, global volume increased particularly in

Asia and Europe. The U.S. auto industry was profitable in every year since 1955, except those years following U.S. recessions and involvement in wars. U.S. auto industry profits suffered from 1971-1973 during the Vietnam War, during the recession in the late 1970s which impacted auto industry profits from 1981-83, during and after the Gulf War when industry profits declined from 1991-93, and during the Iraq War from 2001-03 and 2006-09. During these periods the companies incurred much legacy debts. Facing financial losses, the Big Three have idled (sic) many factories, and drastically reduced employment levels. GM spun off many of its employees in certain divisions into independent companies, including American Axle in 1994 and Delphi in 1999. Ford spun off Visteon in 2000. The spinoffs and other parts makers have shared Detroit's downturns, as have the U.S.-owned plants in Canada. Altogether the parts makers employ 416,000 people in the U.S. and Canada. General Motors alone estimated to have lost $51 billion in the three years before the 2008 financial crisis began. GM is set to reacquire factories from its Delphi subsidiary during its Chapter 11 restructuring . . . . Delphi which was spun off from GM in 1999, filed for Chapter 11 bankruptcy after UAW refused to cut their wages and GM is expected to be liable for a $7 billion shortfall. In order to improve profits, the Detroit automakers made agreements with unions to reduce wages while making pension and healthcare commitments. GM for instance, at one time picked up the entire cost of funding health insurance premiums of its employees, their survivors and GM retirees, as the U.S. did not have a universal healthcare system. [If this did not open the eyes of the American public as to the need for a Universal Healthcare System, such as the Affordable Healthcare Act; as proposed by President Barack Obama: what will?] With most of these plans chronically underfunded in the late 1990s, the companies have tried to provide retirement packages to older employees, and make agreements with the UAW to transfer pension obligations to an independent trust. Nevertheless, non-unionized Japanese automakers, with their younger American workforces (and far fewer American retirees) will continue to enjoy a cost advantage . . . . In September, 2008, the Big Three asked for $50 billion to pay for healthcare expenses and avoid bankruptcy and ensuing layoffs, and Congress worked out a $25 billion loan. By December, President Bush had agreed to an emergency bailout of $17.4 billion to be distributed by the next administration in January and February. In early 2009, the prospect of avoiding bankruptcy by General Motors and Chrysler continued to wane as new financial information about the scale of the 2008 losses came in. Ultimately, poor management and business practices forced Chrysler and General Motors into bankruptcy. Chrysler filed for Chapter 11 bankruptcy protection on May 1, 2009 followed by General Motors a month later." [At the time that President Barack Obama decided to bailout the American Auto Industry, there was much opposition to this initiative especially by the Republican Party. However, on November 6, 2012 President Obama was re-elected to a second term by a populace who approved of his economic stimulus program, thus saving the American Automotive Industry from closing down and causing the workers to be unemployed. At the time of the bailout, the auto industry literally had two weeks before failing. The American Automotive Industry needs to improve on their products. They should try to be more competitive in the world market by retooling and redesigning. There is a lot of space for improvement in areas such as better fuel economy; park assist, GPS and backup cameras, and emergency braking technology to avoid rear-end collisions. It can be done for all American cars at a reasonable price.] (Wikipedia, Automotive Industry Crisis of 2008-2010, 2008)

TARP-CONGRESS AUTHORIZES THE TREASURY DEPARTMENT

(3) Wikipedia asserts that, "The Troubled Asset Relief Program (TARP) is a program of the United States Government to purchase assets and equity from financial institutions to strengthen its financial sector that was signed into law by U.S. President George W. Bush on October 3, 2008. It was a component of the government's measures in 2008 to address the subprime mortgage crisis. The TARP program originally authorized expenditures of $700 billion and was expected to cost the U.S. taxpayers as much as $300 billion. By March3, 2011, the Congressional Budget Office (CBO) stated that total disbursements would be $432 billion and estimated the total cost would be $19 billion. This is significantly less than the taxpayers' cost of the savings and loan crisis of the late 1980's but does not include the cost of other 'bailout' programs (such as the Federal Reserve's Maiden Lane Transactions and the Federal takeover of Fannie Mae and Freddie Mac). The cost of that crises amounted to 3.2 percent of GDP during the Reagan/Bush era, while the GDP percentage of the current crisis cost is estimated at less than 1 percent. While it was once feared the government would be holding companies like GM, AIG, and Citigroup for several years, those companies are preparing to buy back the Treasury's stake and emerge from TARP within a year. Of the $245 billion invested in U.S. banks,

over $169 billion has been paid back, including $13.7 billion in dividends, interest and other income, along with $4 billion in warrant proceeds as of April 2010. AIG is considered 'on track' to pay back $51 billion from divestitures of two units and another $32 billion in securities. TARP allows the United States Department of the Treasury to purchase or to insure up to $700 billion of 'troubled assets,' defined as (A) residential or commercial mortgages and any securities, obligations, or other instruments that are based on or related to such mortgages, that in each case was originated or issued on or before March 14, 2008, the purchase of which the Secretary determines promotes financial market stability; and (B) any other financial instrument that the Secretary, after consultation with the Chairman of the Board of Governors of the Federal Reserve System, determines the purchase of which is necessary to promote financial market stability, but only on transmittal of such determination, in writing, to the appropriate committees of Congress.... The authority of the United States Department of the Treasury to establish and manage TARP under a newly created Office of Financial Stability became law October 3, 2008, the result of an initial proposal that ultimately was passed by Congress as H.R. 1424, enacting the Emergency Economic Stabilization Act of 2008 and several other acts. On October 14, 2008 Secretary of the Treasury Paulson and President Bush separately announced revisions of the TARP program. The Treasury announced their intention to buy senior preferred stock and warrants from the nine largest American banks. The shares would qualify as Tier 1 capital and were non-voting shares. To qualify for this program, the Treasury required participating institutions to meet certain criteria, including: '(1) ensuring that incentive compensation for senior executives does not encourage unnecessary and excessive risks that threaten the value of the financial institution; (2) required clawback of any bonus or incentive compensation paid to a senior executive based on statements of earnings, gains or other criteria that are later proven to be materially inaccurate; (3) prohibition on the financial institution from making any golden parachute payment to a senior executive based on the Internal Revenue Code provision; and (4) agreement not to deduct for tax purposes executive compensation in excess of $500,000 for each senior executive. The Treasury also bought preferred stock and warrants from hundreds of smaller banks, using the first $250 billion allocated to the program. The first allocation of the TARP money was primarily used to buy preferred stock, which is similar to debt in that it gets paid before common equity shareholders. This has led some economists to argue that the plan may be ineffective in inducing banks to lend efficiently.... On November 12, 2008, Secretary of the Treasury Henry Paulson indicated that reviving the securitization market for consumer credit would be a new priority in the second allotment. On December 19, 2008, President Bush used his executive authority to declare that TARP funds may be spent on any program that Secretary of Treasury Henry Paulson deemed necessary to alleviate the financial crisis. On December 31, 2008, the Treasury issued a report reviewing Section 102, the Troubled Assets Insurance Financing Fund, also known as the 'Asset Guarantee Program.' The report indicated that the program would not likely be made 'widely available.' On January 15, 2009, the Treasury issued interim final rules for reporting and record keeping requirements under the executive compensation standards of the Capital Purchase Program (CPP). On January 21, 2009, the Treasury announced new regulations regarding disclosure and mitigation of conflicts of interest in its TARP contracting. On February 5, 2009, the Senate approved changes to the TARP that prohibited firms receiving TARP funds from paying bonuses to their 25 highest-paid employees. The measure was proposed by Christopher Dodd of Connecticut as an amendment to the $900 billion economic stimulus act then waiting to be passed. On February 10, 2009, the newly confirmed Secretary of the Treasury Timothy Geithner outlined his plan to use the remaining $300 billion or so in TARP funds. He intended to direct $50 billion towards foreclosure mitigation and use the rest to help fund private investors to buy toxic assets from banks. Nevertheless, this highly anticipated speech coincided with nearly 5 percent drop in S&P 500 and was criticized for lacking details.... On April 19, the Obama administration outlined the conversion of Bank Bailouts to Equity Share.... <u>Homeownership preservation</u>: When we purchase mortgages and mortgage backed securities, we will look for every opportunity possible to help homeowners. This goal is consistent with other programs—such as HOPE NOW—aimed at working with borrowers, counselors and services to keep people in their homes. In this case, we are working with the Department of Housing and Urban Development to maximize these opportunities to help as many homeowners as possible, while also protecting taxpayers. <u>Executive compensation:</u> The law sets out important requirements regarding executive compensation for firms that participate in the TARP. This team is working hard to define the requirements for financial institutions to participate in three possible scenarios: One, an auction purchase of troubled assets, two, a broad equity of direct purchase program; and three, a case of an intervention to prevent the impending failure of a systematically significant institution.

Compliance: The law establishes important oversight and compliance structures, including establishing an Oversight Board, on-site participation of the General Accounting Office and the creation of a Special Inspector General, with thorough reporting requirements.... One of the most difficult issues facing the Treasury in managing TARP is the pricing of the troubled assets. The Treasury must find a way to price extremely complex and sometimes unwieldy instruments for which a market does not exist. In addition, the pricing must strike a balance between efficiently using public funds provided by the taxpayer and providing adequate assistance to the financial institutions that need it.... The Congressional Budget Office (CBO) uses procedures similar to those specified in the Federal Credit Reform Act (FCRA) to value assets purchased under the TARP. In a report dated February 6, 2009, the Congressional Oversight Panel concluded that the Treasury paid substantially more for the assets it purchased under the TARP than their then current market value. The (COP) found the Treasury paid $254 billion, for which it received assets worth approximately $176 billion for a shortfall of $78 billion. The COP's valuation analysis assumed that 'securities similar to those issued under the TARP were trading in the capital markets at fair values' and employed multiple approaches to cross-check and evaluate the results. The value was estimated for each security as of the time immediately following the announcement by Treasury of its purchase. For example, the COP found that the Treasury bought $25 billion of assets from Citigroup on October 14, 2008, however the actual value was estimated to be $15.5 billion, creating a 38 percent (or $9.5 billion) subsidy.... Recoupment: This provision was a big factor in the eventual passage of the EESA. It gives taxpayers the opportunity to 'be repaid.' The recoupment provision requires the Director of the Office of Management and Budget to submit a report on TARP's financial status to Congress five years after its enactment. If TARP has not been able to recoup its outlays through the sale of the assets, the Act requires the President to submit a plan to Congress to recoup the losses from the financial industry. Theoretically, this prevents TARP from adding to the national debt. The use of the term 'financial industry' in the provision leaves open the possibility that such a plan would involve the entire financial sector rather than only those institutions that availed themselves of TARP."

(Wikipedia, Troubled Asset Relief Program, 2011)

REGIONS RETURNS TARP MONEY

(4) Reporter Jeffrey Sparshott writes, "WASHINGTON—Regions Financial Corp. repaid the U.S. Treasury $3.5 billion, allowing it to exit the federal government bailout program. "REGIONS" was the biggest bank remaining in the Troubled Asset Relief Program, or TARP. With Wednesday's repayment, TARP's bank programs have turned an $18 billion profit, Treasury said. Even with the returns on bank programs, the Congressional Budget Office estimates that overall TARP will end up costing taxpayers $32 billion. The cost stems largely from assistance to American International Group Inc., aid to the automotive industry and grant programs aimed at avoiding foreclosures. Still, Wednesday's repayment shows that the government is accelerating its winding down of TARP. Last week, Treasury sold stakes in seven smaller banks—all at a small loss on the initial investment. The government still owns stakes in roughly 350 banks more than three years after TARP's launch and expects to exit many of those at a discount. Regions—in addition to the $3.5 billion repayment, has paid Treasury $593 million in dividends. Treasury said it still holds warrants to purchase common stock in the bank, the sale of which will provide further returns. 'This repayment is another milestone in our effort to wind down TARP and provides an additional profit for taxpayers on the program's investment in banks,' Assistant Secretary of Financial Stability Tim Massad said. Treasury invested $3.5 billion in Birmingham, Ala., bank in November 2008. Regions repurchased preferred stock that Treasury had held as collateral. 'On an annual ongoing basis, the repurchase eliminates the payment of $175 million in dividends on these securities,' Regions said in a statement. Regions on Monday completed the sale of Brokerage Morgan Keegan & Co. to Raymond James Financial Inc., generating $1.2 billion in proceeds and allowing it to make the lump payment to Treasury." (Sparshott, April 05, 2012)

INSIDER TRADING

(5) A report on Wikipedia states, "Insider-Trading is the trading of a corporation's stock or other securities (e.g. bonds or stock options) by individuals with potential access to non-public information about the company. In most countries, trading by corporate insiders such as officers, key employees, directors, and large shareholders may be legal, if this trading is done in a way that does not take advantage of non-public information. However, the term is frequently used to

refer to a practice in which an insider or a related party trades based on material non-public information obtained during the performance of the insider's duty at the corporation, or otherwise in breach of a fiduciary or other relationship of trust and confidence or where the non-public information was misappropriated from the company . . . . Illegal insider trading is believed to raise the cost of capital for securities issuers, thus decreasing overall economic growth. However, it is relatively easy for insiders to capture insider-trading like gains through the use of transactions known as 'open market repurchases.' Such transactions are legal and generally encouraged by regulators through safeharbors against insider trading liability . . . . Legal trades by insiders are common, as employees of publicly traded corporations often have stock or stock options. These trades are made public in the United States through Securities and Exchange Commission filings, mainly Form 4. Prior to 2001, U.S. law restricted trading such that insiders mainly traded during windows when their inside information was public, such as soon after earnings releases . . . . Rules against insider trading on material non-public information exist in most jurisdictions around the world, though the details and the efforts to enforce them vary considerably. Sections 16(b) and 10(b) of the Securities and Exchange Act of 1934 directly and indirectly address insider trading. Congress enacted this act after the stock market crash of 1929. The United States is generally viewed as having the strictest laws against illegal insider trading and makes the most serious efforts to enforce them . . . . Liability for inside trading violations cannot be avoided by passing on the information in an 'I scratch your back, you scratch mine' or quid pro quo arrangement, as long as the person receiving the information knew or should have known that the information was company property. It should be noted that when allegations of a potential inside deal occur, all parties that may have been involved are at risk of being found guilty . . . . A newer view of insider trading, the 'misappropriation theory,' is now part of U.S. law. It states that anyone who misappropriates (steals) information from their employer and trades on that information in any stock (either the employer's stock or the company's competitor stocks) is guilty of insider trading . . . . Proving that someone has been responsible for a trade can be difficult, because traders may try to hide behind nominees, offshore companies, and other proxies. Nevertheless, the U.S. Securities and Exchange Commission prosecutes over 50 cases each year, with many being settled administratively out of court. The SEC and several stock exchanges actively monitor trading, looking for suspicious activity . . . . Members of Congress are exempted from insider trading laws and thus can act on information they are bound to gain in the course of their congressional activities, although house rules may consider it unethical. A 2004 study found that stock sales and purchases by Senators outperformed the market by 12.3% per year. Peter Schweizer points out several examples of insider trading by members of Congress, including action taken by Spencer Bachus following a private, behind-the-doors meeting on the evening of September 18, 2008 when Hank Paulson and Ben Bernanke informed members of Congress about the imminent financial crisis. Bachus then shorted stocks the next morning and cashed in his profits within a week. Also attending the same meeting were Senator Dick Durbin and John Boehner; the same day (trade effective the next day). Durbin sold mutual-fund shares worth $42,696, and reinvested it all with Warren Buffett. Also the same day (trade effective the next day), Congressman Boehner cashed out of an equity mutual fund. (Wikipedia, Insider Trading)

INSIDER BILL PASSES WITH NEW BACKERS

(6) Michael Rothfeld and Jason Zweig states, "After a six-year effort, the House of Representatives passed legislation that would formally ban insider trading by Congress, along the way picking up support from some surprising backers—lawmakers who actively traded stocks. [Of course there would be surprising backers. Members of Congress are no idiots. They know that the populace is watching their every move in an election year to evaluate whether they are there for their own sweet interests or those of their constituents. The two die-hard, do-nothing republican representatives that did not back this bill ought to be ashamed of themselves.] A total of 286 House members from both political parties co-sponsored a bill known as the Stop Trading on Congressional Knowledge, or Stock Act. The legislation, which was first proposed in 2006 but drew no more than 15 sponsors in earlier years, passed 417-2 Thursday and will be reconciled with a Senate version approved last week. There is nothing wrong with members of Congress trading stock. The Stock Act won't prevent them from buying and selling shares, and there is no suggestion that any sponsor engaged in insider trading. [This is laughable and hard to believe. If as suggested, no representative have ever traded on insider-information, then why the pressing need for the passing of a Stock Act? And why did it take six years to be legislated?] But some members of Congress

who trade say they are aware of potential pitfalls because they may have access to nonpublic information about government contracts, developments in their districts and other market-moving intelligence. 'I've always believed Newport News shipyard stock (now part of Huntington Ingalls Industries Inc.) is a good investment,' said Rep, Robert C. 'Bobby' Scott, a Virginia Democrat whose district includes the shipyard, which does work for the Navy and at times has been owned by public companies. 'But I never bought any stock because I'm always privy to information that's non-public . . . . The majority of 535 members of Congress didn't trade much in 2010, according to data compiled by the center for Responsive Politics, a Washington non-profit group. Only 392 members reported itemized transactions and just 86 listed more than 40. Many of the reported trades were in Bonds, Mutual Funds, Bank Instruments and other investments unlikely to be gained by inside information . . . . The two Congressmen who voted against the bill, Rep. John Campbell (R-Calif.) and Rep. Rob Woodall (R-Ga.) also invest in stocks, their disclosure forms show. A spokeswoman for Mr. Woodall didn't respond to a request for comment. Mr. Campbell said in a statement that he found the bill 'ambiguous' and that it could cause members and constituents 'to break the law by simply asking or answering a question about the prospects of federal legislation.' Mr. Campbell's spokesman said Mr. Campbell inherited the stocks after his father died and sold them in 2006 to avoid conflicts. (Rothfeld, 02/10/2012)

BAN ON INSIDER TRADING BY CONGRESS BECOMES LAW

(7) Finally, it's now the law, but not all members of Congress support the Insider Trading Bill or Stock Act. Remember, members of Congress are only human. As are the greedy and unscrupulous executives and lobbyists you will be reading about in chapter three.

Jared A. Favole writes, "President Barak Obama signed a law Wednesday, April 4, 2012 cracking down on insider trading in Congress. He said among the country's most 'cherished' notions is that everyone should play by the same rules. 'It's the notion that the powerful shouldn't get to create one set of rules for themselves, and another set of rules for everybody else,' he said before signing the Stop Trading on Congressional Knowledge, or Stock Act. The law comes after a six-year effort by a group of House law makers to ban insider trading by members of Congress. Law makers from both parties attended the signing, including Sen. Scott Brown (R, Mass.), Rep. David Cicilline (D. RI.) and Rep. Sean Duffy (R. Wis.) Rep. Louise Slaughter, a Democrat from New York who introduced legislation to ban insider trading in 2006, wasn't in attendance. She broke her leg, the President said, but was proud of the law. Insider trading is illegal already, but whether the law could be applied to Capitol Hill was a matter of dispute. (Favole, April 5, 2012)

INVESTORS—BEWARE OF PRE-IPO SECONDARY MARKETS

(8) Reporters Randall Smith and Jean Eaglesham report that, "Federal regulators are cracking down on an obscure but booming market for trading shares in companies before they go public. The Securities and Exchange Commission brought charges against two money managers, alleging they misled and overcharged investors on funds formed to buy shares of Facebook Inc., Twitter Inc. and other social-media companies. A so-called secondary market in these companies' private shares has grown rapidly as more investors seek to buy into the companies before their initial public offerings, hoping to profit later from a 'pop' in the stock price after the IPO. The allegations by the SEC mark the first major regulatory blow to the market, which the agency says emerged in 2009 and which industry participants say has been fueled lately on the participation of a Facebook IPO in the coming months. The actions show regulators are concerned that the markets are murky and fall short of the types of disclosures that typically accompany public-market investments. 'The newly emerging secondary marketplace for pre-IPO stock presents risk for even savvy investors' said Marc Fagel, director of the SEC's Francisco regional office. The crackdown comes as Congress considers a new law that the SEC fears could fuel fraud in the shares of closely held companies. The jobs bill, expected to be agreed on this month by lawmakers, is designed to help small businesses raise capital by easing many existing controls on fund-raising processes such as IPOs. In the private-shares market, former employees and early investors mostly in technology companies sell shares to investors through a network of brokers and fund-companies that has sprung up in the past few years. Dozens of investment vehicles have been created with the hard-to-obtain shares. Trading volume of private shares doubled last year to $9.3 billion, according to Nyppex Holdings LLC, which trades and participates

in the market for illiquid securities. By comparison, 2011 volume of stocks in the Wilshire 5000, a broad measure of those that trade on all U.S. exchanges, was $35 trillion. The SEC probe of the private market intensified after a $1.5 billion private placement of Facebook shares was orchestrated by Goldman Sachs Group Inc. in January 2011, illustrating both the extent of investor interest in the stock and its skyrocketing valuation, at the time $50 billion. Amid the frenzy over the Facebook IPO, the market for private shares have become 'a bit of a free-for-all,' said analyst Max Wolff, who does research on private-market stocks at Green Crest Capital in New York. He said the SEC actions could help reduce 'some of the worst practices' in the business and 'put the brakes on the runaway market.' The SEC allege that Frank Mazzola, Felix Investments LLC and Facie Libre Management Associates LLC earned secret commissions on the sale of Facebook shares and stakes in the funds, in addition to the 5% commissions disclosed to investors. 'The hidden charges essentially raised the prices paid by the firms' investors for Facebook stock,' the SEC said. Mr. Mazzola's funds raised a total of $56 million, the SEC said. Mr. Mazzola declined to comment. Jack Hewitt of McCarter and English LLP, a lawyer acting for Mr. Mazzola, Felix and Facie Libre, didn't return calls and emails seeking comment. Earlier in a filing with regulators, Mr. Mazzola said he had received warnings in August and September 2011 that he was under scrutiny by the SEC and the Financial Industry Regulatory Authority, or FINRA. Mr. Mazzola said at the time he would 'aggressively defend himself in this matter.' FINRA on Wednesday fined Felix, Mr. Mazzola and two other Felix employees a total of $330,000 for allegedly breaching the rules on how investments can be sold in their promotion of the Facebook funds. Finra allege the company pitched the funds to more than 1,000 people, 'often through mass mailings of boilerplate emails.' The SEC also alleged in an administrative action that Lawrence Albukerk and his firm EB Financial Group LLC obtained hidden compensation of two funds that raised $15.4 million to buy Facebook stakes by using an entity controlled by his wife to buy the Facebook stock, then buying the assets at an undisclosed markup for the fund. Mr. Albukerk and EB Financial consented to an order finding they violated SEC rules; they agreed to pay $310,499 in settling the case, and neither admitted nor denied the SEC's findings. Mr. Albukerk's wife wasn't charged. A spokesman for Mr. Albukerk and EB Financial said the firm is 'pleased to put this matter behind us,' adding that the fees in question were 'legally earned' and that each investor's stake 'appears profitable.' Also on Wednesday, Shares Post Inc., one of the biggest firms matching sellers and buyers of closely held shares such as Facebook, paid $80,000 to settle an administrative action filed by the SEC concerning its failure to register as a broker-dealer. The firm, which registered as a broker-dealer last year, said in a statement it neither confirmed nor denied the agency's factual findings or legal conclusions. Shares Post said it has so far completed more than 1,500 transactions without a single customer complaint being made to the SEC or Finra. In Washington the controversial jobs bill has already been passed by the House and is backed by President Barack Obama. But Mary Schapiro, SEC chairwoman, warned in a six page letter to Congress this week that she was concerned the bill could eliminate important protections for investors, even in some relatively large public companies. An SEC spokesman said the timing of the actions had nothing to do with the agency's concerns about the legislation, which the Senate is expected to vote on within days. The SEC is still reviewing whether to relax the 500-share-holder rule, requiring companies to disclose a swath of financial information once they have 500 or more registered shareholders".

(Smith, 03-15-2012)

FACEBOOK SHARES START TRADING

(9) Facebook founder Mark Zuckerberg rang the opening bell for the first day of trading Facebook, which was listed on the NASDAQ Stock Market. The ringing of the opening bell was done remotely from Facebook's headquarters in Menlo Park, California. The company which was created in a college dorm at Harvard quickly grew to be the third largest public-offering stock. Facebook's opening trade was delayed, which normally was to be expected, in order to facilitate the matching of a large volume of buy and sell orders in an opening block-sale.

There was great hype that Facebook would have an opening price of $110.00 per share. However, after the bids and offers were paired off electronically, the shocking surprise to all was an opening price of $43.00 per share. At the close of the first day of trading, Facebook shares closed just above $38.00 per share—down approximately 35% below the pre-IPO suggested offering price.

GOLDMAN PLAYS DAMAGE CONTROL

(10) Investors, please read and understand that wishing upon a star and giving your hard earned cash to so-called financial gurus with their get-rich-quick Ponzi schemes will only cause you to be financially bankrupt, and licking your wounds with sleepless nights. The excerpts presented may at a glance be interpreted as boring Wall Street mumbo-jumbo, but if carefully read and understood, will save many of bleeding hearts. It will be beneficial to the not so savvy investor to educate themselves about Stock Markets, types of stocks, graphs and charts, and to meet with a qualified financial advisor. Perhaps you can consider investing in no-load funds, with only a reasonable fee and no commission. If you have the financial clout you may also invest in real estate.

> In a report by Liz Rappaport and David Enrich, they reported that: "Goldman Sachs Group Inc. said it will examine claims by an employee who quit Wednesday that executives 'callously' talk about 'ripping their clients off' in order to make more money for the securities firm. The pledge was part of a day-long scramble by the New York Company to contain potential damage from the public attack. The employee, 33-year-old Greg Smith, wrote in the New York Times that he had decided to walk away from his 12-year career at Goldman because of the firm's 'toxic and destructive' culture—a 1,270 word denunciation that ricocheted around the world in sharply divided tweets, Facebook comments and blog posts.
> At Goldman, the op-ed prompted anger toward Mr. Smith and new introspection among executives stung by persistent outside criticism of the company since the financial crisis began. Unlike previous incidents in which Goldman seemed to be caught flat-footed, company officials quickly launched a public-relations counteroffensive Wednesday that minimized Mr. Smith's role at the firm.
> In a memo to employees, Goldman Chairman and Chief Executive Lloyd C. Blankfein and President Gary D. Cohn wrote that Mr. Smith was one 'of nearly 12,000 vice presidents' among more than 30,000 employees at the company.
> Mr. Smith was described in the op-ed as executive director and head of Goldman's equity derivatives business in Europe, the Middle East and Africa. Mr. Smith couldn't be reached for comment. He left his London office after work Tuesday and resigned shortly before the article was published, according to a person familiar with the situation. Mr. Smith, who had been a Goldman vice president for six years, posted a

link to the article on his Facebook page. [Was he truly a conscionable, honest whistleblower or was he a disgruntled worker having received a shrunken bonus and possibly passed over for promotion as hinted in their comment.]

Messrs. Blankfein and Cohn said what Mr. Smith wrote does 'not reflect our values, our culture and how the vast majority of people at Goldman Sachs think about the firm and the work it does on behalf of our clients.' They said Goldman officials would 'examine carefully' the issues that were raised by Mr. Smith. The company has tried to contact him for more information about his accusations, including that he saw five managing directors call their clients 'Muppets' in the past year. 'Muppet' is a British slang term for 'idiot' and is sometimes used on Wall Street to denigrate an opposing trader. As part of the internal review, Goldman officials began talking Wednesday to Mr. Smith's former bosses and colleagues in London, hoping to determine whether he raised any concerns with them, a company spokesman said. Mr. Blankfein and other executives also spent much of the day discussing the matter with Goldman directors, shareholders and clients.

Goldman shares fell 3.4 % or $4.17, to $120.37 in New York Stock Exchange composite trading at 4 p.m. after gaining $7.55 on Tuesday. Shares of the rival Morgan Stanley also slipped. At this point, it is unlikely that Mr. Smith's complaint will be referred to Goldman's legal and compliance departments or to a group of top Goldman executives responsible for reviewing serious incidents or industry matters of concern.

While Goldman worked to counter Mr. Smith's screed, some executives and other employees said that his words felt like an extreme version of their own concerns about the company. The grip of Goldman's strong partnership culture has loosened since the firm went public in 1999. And even some of the company's staunchest defenders feel beleaguered by outrage over its role in the financial crisis.

Morale also is suffering because last year was the least profitable for Goldman since 2008, and many employee bonuses shrank by at least half. Some employees in London and New York got no bonus for last year, according to people familiar with the situation. Mr. Smith, who was born in South Africa, is known inside Goldman as a quiet, hard worker who didn't complain openly about life at the firm or how it treated clients, according to people familiar with the matter.

Before quitting, Mr. Smith was responsible for selling equity derivatives to European hedge funds, asset managers and other clients. In revenue-generating positions, it is unusual for Goldman vice presidents to keep that title for as long as Mr. Smith did, according to Goldman executives. Such executives usually are promoted to managing director or leave the firm for more lucrative jobs elsewhere. (Rappaport & Enrich, March 15, 2012)

OCCUPY WALL STREET—2011

(11) Occupy Wall Street is a movement borne out of the rage by the masses of the poor, the disappearing middle class, the homeless, the hungry, the destitute, the jobless, the hopeless, immigrant injustices, and the downright forlorn. This leaderless passive resistance movement began in New York, U.S.A. on September 17, 2011 with demonstrators in the financial district. The movement mimicked that of the uprising in Tahrir Square, Egypt. The demonstrators of Occupy Wall Street Movement branded themselves as the 99% desperately looking for jobs during the serious economic downturn in the United States. About 25 million people were unemployed; millions lost their homes to "foreclosures and short-sales" principally brought about by the illicit activities and greed of Banking Executives and other Mega Corporations trading on the major Stock Exchanges. When "Wall Street" is mentioned, some believe the reference is just about the New York Stock Exchange; but in fact in the broader scheme of things it encompasses the New York Stock Exchange, the American Stock Exchange, the NASD and others.

The movement had started with a handful of protestors at the lower Manhattan Plaza, known as Zuccotti Park. They were outraged by the big divide between that of the 99% masses, versus the income buildup of the 1% of large corporations and their executives making illegal trades, money laundering, and Mortgage Bankers ripping off the populace with their dishonesty, and unconventional loan practices. Similar demonstrations sprang up in cities throughout the U.S. and also in capital cities throughout the world; that suffered an economic crisis.

Congress on the other hand, instead of doing the work of "We the People," they aligned themselves with the big lobbyists and the rest of the 1%. The salaries of Members of Congress had grown by 15%, while middle class salaries plummeted by 8%. The population is now demanding justice from Congress and no longer willing to tolerate corporate greed, and the influence of lobbyists; that the 1% represents. The 99% is looking and hoping for real economic empowerment and progress.

Immigrant injustices are also of major concern; they are demanding an end to wage disparity for suspected undocumented workers, unconscionable detentions and deportations, and separation of family units among Hispanics.

In order to fully appreciate the causes for the rage, and demand by the Occupy Wall Street Movement for better economic parity and the end to corporate greed; the excerpts in the next chapter should be thoroughly examined.

People who once owned their homes and had jobs used to support "food pantries" throughout the country. Today those same residents and their dependents are homeless and are eating at those same food pantries. Where is the middle class? They are most of them among the poor and unfortunate.

Wikipedia Encyclopedia documents that, "On December 6, 2011, Occupy Homes, an offshoot of Occupy Wall Street, embarked on a 'national day of action' to protest the mistreatment of homeowners by big banks, who they say made billions of dollars off the housing bubble by offering predatory loans and indulging in practices that allegedly took advantage of consumers. In more than two dozen cities across the nation the movement took on the housing crisis by re-occupying foreclosed homes, disrupting bank auctions and blocking evictions.

On September 17, 2012, protesters returned to Zuccotti Park to mark the one year anniversary of the beginning of the occupation. On September 26, administrators of the University of California agreed to pay out roughly $1 million to end a lawsuit brought by UC Davis students who were pepper sprayed by police at a protest on November 18, 2011. Students had gathered to protest against rising tuition costs and reduced services". (Encyclopedia, 2012)

BBA LIBOR

This is undeniably the biggest scandal in recent times, and another shot in the arm for the Occupy Wall Street Movement. These kinds of fleecing and unconscionable trade practices undermines the confidence of nations, destroying investors, tax-payers and mortgage holders, and gives no hope to small business owners; who are all affected by Libor Rates. This kind of market manipulation perpetuates public distrust and could lead to a social revolution. Since all the major banks in the U.S. participate in setting the Libor Rates—their criminal involvement remains suspect.

(12) Wikipedia states, "The London Interbank Offered Rate is the average interest rate estimated by leading banks in London that they would be charged if borrowing from other banks. It is usually abbreviated to LIBOR, or more officially to BBA LIBOR (for British Bankers Association Libor) or the trade mark BBALIBOR. It is a benchmark, along with Euribor, for interest rates all over the world. Libor rates are calculated for different lending periods; overnight, one week, one

month, two months, six months, etc., and published daily after 11 a.m. (London time) by Thomson Reuters. Many financial institutions, mortgage lenders and credit card agencies set their own rates relative to (and typically higher than Libor. In 1984, it became apparent that an increasing number of banks were trading actively in a variety of relatively new market instruments, notably interest rate swaps, foreign currency options and forward rate agreements. While recommending that such instruments brought more business and greater depth to the London Interbank market, bankers worried that future growth could be inhibited unless a measure of uniformity was introduced. In October 1984, the British Bankers Association (BBA)—working with other parties, such as the Bank of England—established various working parties, which eventually culminated in the production of the BBA standard for interest rate swaps, or 'BBAIRS' terms. Part of this standard including the fixing of BBA interest-settlement rates, the predecessor of BBA Libor. From September 2 1985, the BBAIRS terms became standard market practice. BBA Libor fixings did not commence officially before January1, 1986. Before that date, however, some rates were fixed for a trial period commencing in December 1984. Member banks are international in scope, with more than sixty nations represented among its 223 members and 37 associated professional firms (as of 2008) . . . . The definition of Libor is amplified as follows: (I) the rate at which each bank submits must be formed from that bank's perception of its cost of funds in the interbank market. (II) Contributions must represent rates formed in London and not elsewhere. (III) Contributions must be for the currency concerned, not the cost of producing one currency by borrowing in another currency and accessing the required currency via the foreign exchange markets. (IV) The rates must be submitted by members of staff at a bank with primary responsibility for management of a bank's cash, rather than a bank's derivative book. (V) The definition of 'funds' is; unsecured interbank cash or cash raised through primary issuance of interbank Certificates of Deposit . . . . Libor is often used as a rate of reference for pound sterling and other currencies, including US dollar, euro, Japanese yen, Swiss franc, Canadian dollar, Australian dollar, Swedish krona, Danish krone, and New Zealand dollar. In the 1990s, the yen Libor was influenced by credit problems affecting some of the contributor banks. Six-month USD Libor is used as an index for some US mortgages. In the UK, the three-month GBP Libor is used for some mortgages—especially for those with adverse credit history. The Chicago Mercantile Exchange's Eurodollar contracts are based on three-month US dollar Libor rates. They are the world's most heavily traded short term interest rate futures contracts and extend up to ten years. Shorter term maturities trade on the Singapore Exchange in Asian time.... On Thursday, May 29, 2008, The Wall Street Journal (WSJ) released a controversial study suggesting that banks might have understating borrowing costs they reported for Libor during the 2008 credit crunch. Such underreporting could have created an impression that banks could borrow from other banks more cheaply than they could in reality. It could also have made the banking system or specific contributing bank appear healthier than it was during the 2008 credit crunch. For example, the study found that rates at which one major bank (Citi-group) 'said it could borrow dollars for three months were about 0.87 percentage point lower than the rate calculated using default-insurance data.'.... On 28 February 2012, it was revealed that the SEC was conducting a criminal investigation into LIBOR abuse. Among the abuses being investigated, was the possibility that traders were in direct communication with bankers before the rates were set, thus allowing them an unprecedented amount of insider knowledge into global instruments. LIBOR underpins approximately $350 trillion in derivatives. One trader's messages indicated that for each basis point (0.01%) that LIBOR was moved, those involved could net 'about a couple of million dollars'. On June 27, 2012, Barclays Bank was fined $200 million by The Commodity Futures Trading Commission, $160 million by the United States Department of Justice and 59.5 million pounds sterling by the (FSA) Financial Services Authority for attempted manipulation of the LIBOR and EURIBOR rates. The United States Department of Justice and Barclays officially agreed that 'the manipulation of the submissions affected the fixed rate on some occasions'. On July 2, 2012, Marcus Agius, chairman of Barclays, resigned from the position following the interest rate rigging scandal. Bob Diamond, the chief executive officer of Barclays, resigned on July 3, 2012. Marcus Agius will fill his post until a replacement is found. Jerry Del Missier, Chief Operating Officer of Barclays, also resigned, as a casualty of the scandal. Del Missier subsequently admitted that he had instructed his subordinates to submit falsified LIBORs to the British Bankers Association. By July 4, 2012, the breadth of the scandal was evident and became the topic of analysis on news and financial programs that attempted to explain the importance of the scandal. On July 6, 2012, it was announced that the U.K. Serious Fraud Office had also opened a criminal investigation into the attempted manipulation of interest rates". (Wikipedia, Libor, 2012)

Chapter Four

EXCERPTS ON THE GREED OF BANKERS AND TRADERS ON WALL STREET

Investors on Main Street may wonder what these excerpts have to do with the man in the Street. Well, it has a lot to do with the economy and the effects on all our lives. These Brokerage Houses and their Representatives trade on the major Stock Exchanges, and some Stocks and Derivatives are dually listed and traded. Greed for money by illicit means, grandiose bonuses, lobbyists, and kickbacks mute the public's cry for honesty, justice and prosperity; and reinforces the obnoxious behaviors of the Wall Street Gangsters and Banksters. These excerpts are relevant for improving the knowledge of the less sophisticated investors, showing the relevancy of various agencies in the sphere of Stock and Option trading; and the often greed and cover-up by company executives.

Initially the "Securities and Exchange Commission" made frequent visits to the major exchanges; investigating and scrutinizing all major complaints of unfair trade practices. However, after the Bernie Madoff scandal the "Securities and Exchange Commission" was apparently blamed by the Federal Government for being less vigilant by their presence and perhaps in their investigative procedures.

To put it in mild language—Wall Street has abused, deceived, and insulted the American Society. ENRON was known as the seventh largest American Corporation and America's largest bankruptcy scandal, second to none. On Wall Street, it was said that the second space was a toss-up between

WorldCom, and Bernie Madoff who was exposed as the single biggest scam artist (known as the Ponzi Scheme) of the modern brokerage institutions. However, according to Wall Street gossip, there were a lot of scam artists big and small, who were never challenged nor investigated and fined or suspended. Other high profile individuals and companies that were not so fortunate to slip pass scrutiny were Michael Milkin, Ivan Boesky, Charles H. Keating Jr., AIG, Dennis Levine, TARP, Falcone, Lehman Brothers and of course Solyndra and its declaration of bankruptcy. Perhaps this explained why the Occupy Wall Street Movement was born and spread to other American cities, and other cities of other countries. As though that was not enough, there was John Corzine's "MF Global" misuse of investors' funds, and the filing of Chapter 11 Bankruptcy. Will greed and misuse of investors' funds ever stop? Well, this has gone on for ages and will continue for time to come. Let all national and international investors, young and old, be enlightened, be cautious, and be aware!! Here are a number of sensational highlighted excerpts on illicit trading and greed. This list of indicted unscrupulous offenders could easily be seen as elite members of a Financial Mafia.

ENRON CORPORATION—BANKRUPTCY

Let's begin by examining ENRON, a company with executives that thought they could do all wrong and not have to answer to anyone. Here is a company that Fortune Magazine recognized as the most innovative company in America. While Enron's stock prices spiraled theoretically, the stock in reality was plummeting in the red. Enron also known as the Valhalla Scandal became a financial fairyland:

(1) Wikipedia states that, "Enron Corporation was an American energy, commodities, and services company, based in Huston, Texas. Before its bankruptcy on December 2, 2001, Enron employed approximately 22,000 staff and was one of the world's leading electricity, natural gas, communications, and pulp and paper companies, with claimed revenues of nearly $101 billion in 2000. At the end of 2001, it was revealed that its reported financial condition was sustained substantially by institutionalized, systematic, and creatively planned accounting fraud known as the 'Enron Scandal'. Enron has since become a popular symbol of willful corporate fraud and corruption. These scandals also brought into question the accounting practices and activities of many corporations throughout the United States and was a factor in the creation of the Sarbanes-Oxley Act of 2002. The scandal also affected the wider business world by causing the dissolution of the Arthur

Andersen accounting firm. Enron filed for bankruptcy protection in the Southern District of New York in late 2001 and selected Weil, Gotshal & Manges as its bankruptcy counsel. It emerged from bankruptcy in November 2004, pursuant to a court approved plan of reorganization, after one of the biggest and most complex bankruptcy cases in U.S. history. A new board of directors changed the name of Enron to Enron Creditors Recovery Corp., and focused on reorganizing and liquidating certain operations and assets of the pre-bankruptcy Enron. On September 7, 2006, Enron sold Prisma Energy International Inc., its last remaining business, to Ashmore Energy International Ltd. (now AEI). In 1990, Enron finance CEO Jeff Skilling hired Andrew Fastow, who was well acquainted with the burgeoning deregulated energy market Skilling wanted to exploit. In 1993, Fastow set to work establishing numerous limited liability special purposes entities (common business practice); however it also allowed Enron to place liability so that it would not appear in its accounts, allowing it to maintain a robust and generally growing stock price and thus keeping its critical investment grade credit ratings. As was later discovered, many of Enron's recorded assets and profits were inflated or even wholly fraudulent and nonexistent. Debts and losses were put into entities formed 'offshore' that were not included in the firm's financial statements, and other sophisticated and arcane financial transactions between Enron and related companies were used to take unprofitable entities of the company's books. The Enron Scandal, revealed in October 2001, eventually led to the bankruptcy of the Enron Corporation, an American Energy Company based in Houston, Texas, and the dissolution of Arthur Andersen, which was one of the five largest audit and accountancy partnerships in the world. In addition to being the largest bankruptcy organization in American history at the time, Enron was attributed as the biggest audit failure. Enron was formed in 1985 by Kenneth Lay after merging Houston Natural Gas and InterNorth. Several years later, when Jeffrey Skilling was hired, he developed a staff of executives that, through the use of accounting loopholes, special purposes entities and poor financial reporting, were able to hide billions in debt from failed deals and projects. Shareholders lost nearly $11 billion when Enron's stock price, which hit a high of US$90 per share in mid-2000, plummeted to less than $1 by the end of November 2001. The U.S. Securities and Exchange Commission (SEC) began an investigation, and rival Houston competitor Dynergy offered to purchase the company at a fire sale price. The deal fell through, and on December 2, 2001, Enron filed for bankruptcy under

Chapter 11 of the United States Bankruptcy Code. Enron's $63.4 billion in assets made it the largest corporate bankruptcy in U.S. history until WorldCom's bankruptcy the following year. Many executives at Enron were indicted for a variety of charges and were later sentenced to prison. Enron's nontransparent financial statements did not clearly depict its operations and finances with shareholders and analysts. Enron made it a habit of booking costs of cancelled projects as assets, with the rational that no official letter had stated that the project was cancelled. This method was known as 'the snowball', and although it was initially dictated that snowballs stay under $90 million, it was later extended to $200 million." . . . "Main Article: The Trial of Kenneth Lay and Jeffrey Skilling. Fastow and his wife, Lea, pleaded guilty to charges against them. Fastow was initially charged with 98 counts of fraud. Money laundering, insider trading, and conspiracy, among other crimes. Fastow pleaded guilty to two charges of conspiracy and was and was sentenced to ten years with no parole in a plea bargain to testify against Lay, Skilling, and Causey. Lea was indicted on six felony counts, but prosecutors later dropped them in favor of a single misdemeanor tax charge. Lea was sentenced to one year for helping her husband hide income from the government. Lay and Skilling went on trial for their part in the Enron scandal in January 2006. The 53-count, 65-page indictment covers a broad range of financial crimes, including bank fraud, making false statements to banks and auditors, securities fraud, wire fraud, money laundering, conspiracy, and insider trading. District Judge Sim Lake had previously denied motions by the defendants to hold separate trials and to move the case out of Houston, where the defendants argued the negative publicity surrounding Enron's demise would make it impossible to get a fair trial. On May 25, 2006, the jury in the Lay and Skilling trial returned its verdicts. Skilling was convicted of 19 of 28 counts of securities fraud and wire fraud and acquitted on the remaining nine, including charges of insider trading. He was sentenced to 24 years and 4 months in prison. Lay pleaded not guilty to the eleven criminal charges, and claimed that he was misled by those around him. He attributed the main cause for the company's fall to Fastow. Lay was convicted of six counts of securities and wire fraud for which he had been tried, and he faced a total sentence of up to 45 years in prison. However, before sentencing could be scheduled, Lay died on July 5, 2006. At the time of his death, the SEC had been seeking more than $90million from Lay in addition to civil fines. The case surrounding Lay's wife, Linda, is a different one. She sold roughly 500,000 shares of Enron ten minutes to thirty minutes before the information that Enron was collapsing went public on November 28, 2001. Linda was never charged with any of the events related to Enron.... All told, sixteen people pleaded guilty for crimes committed at the company, and five others including four former Merrill Lynch employees, were found guilty. Eight former Enron executives testified—the star witness being Fastow—against Lay and Skilling, his former bosses. Another was Kenneth Price, the former chief of Enron Corp.'s high-speed internet unit, who cooperated and whose testimony helped convict Skilling and Lay. In June 2007, he received a 27-month sentence.... Employers and Shareholders—Enron's shareholders lost $74 billion in the four years before the company's bankruptcy ($40 to $45 billion was attributed to fraud). As Enron had nearly $67 billion that it owed creditors, employees and shareholders received limited, if any, assistance aside from severance from Enron. To pay its creditors, Enron held auctions to sell assets including art, photographs, logo signs, and its pipelines. More than 20,000 of Enron's former employees in May 2004 won a suit of $85 million for compensation of $2 billion that was lost from their pensions. From the settlement, the employees each received about $3,100. The following year, investors received another settlement from several banks of $4.2 billion. In September 2008, a $7.2 billion settlement from a $40 billion law-suit was plaintiff, University of California (UC), and 1.5 million individuals and groups. UC's law firm Coughlin Stoia Geller Rudman and Robbins, received $688 million in fees, the highest in a U.S. securities fraud case. At the distributions, UC announced in a press release 'We are extremely pleased to be returning these funds to the members of the class. Getting here has required a long, challenging effort, but the results for Enron investors are unprecedented." (Wikipedia, Enron Scandal) (Wikipedia, Enron, 2011)

CITICORP SETTLEMENT—FRAUD CHARGES

(2) Chad Bray reports that, "New York—The Securities and Exchange Commission defended its proposed $285 million settlement of fraud charges against Citigroup Inc. over a mortgage-bond deal, calling the agreement 'fair, adequate and reasonable.' Last month, U.S. District

Judge Jed S. Rakoff questioned the government, asking why he should approve the settlement of 'a serious securities fraud' case in which the defendant neither admits nor denies wrongdoing. He ordered both sides to a hearing on Wednesday. In a court filing, Matthew T. Martens, chief litigation counsel in the SEC's Enforcement Division, said the proposed settlement with Citigroup, reached on October 19, was fair and should be approved by Judge Rakoff. 'The proposed consent judgment results in a payment of $285 million by Citigroup,' Mr. Martens said. 'This amount reasonably reflects the monetary relief likely to be available to the commission if successful at a trial on the merits, also taking into account the litigation risks, the benefits of avoiding those risks and the wise allocation of agency resources to serve the interests of investors here, as well as in other matters not before the court.' The SEC had alleged that the New York firm failed to disclose to investors its role in selecting underlying investments in the $1billion mortgage-bond deal called Class V Funding III or that it retained a short position in those assets. The judge asked the SEC to justify why the proposed penalty to be paid by Citigroup is 'less than the one-fifth of the $535 million penalty assessed' in a settlement with Goldman Sachs Group Inc. last year over a complex financial instrument tied to subprime mortgages, named Abacus 2007-AC1. The proposed Citigroup settlement includes a $95 million penalty. In its court filing Monday, the SEC said that the violations alleged against Goldman were 'worthy of a more significant sanction' and the penalty reached with Citigroup reflects the SEC's consideration of the deterrent impact it may have on similar conduct in the future. In its own filing on Monday, Citigroup also said the deal should be approved, noting that the SEC alleged that its employees were accused of negligence in failing to ensure that disclosures to sophisticated investors provided complex information regarding its role in the transaction, rather than intentionally misleading those investors. 'Most significantly, Citigroup did not predict or profit from the sub-prime crisis, the collapse of housing prices, or the collapse of the (collateralized debt obligation) market,' Brad S. Karp, one of the firm's lawyers, said in the documents. 'Precisely to the contrary; over a period of 18 months beginning in late 2007, Citigroup CDO-related losses totaled more than $30 billion—more than any other financial institution in the world.' In its filing, the SEC said potential investor loss could be in excess of $700 million. However, the net profits by Citigroup were at least $160 million." (Bray, Tuesday, November 8, 2011)

CHARLES H. KEATING—VIOLATION OF SECURITIES LAW

(3) Wall Street Journal Staff Reporter states, "LOS ANGELES—The Securities and Exchange Commission formerly notified Charles H. Keating Jr., former chairman of American Continental Corp., parent of insolvent Lincoln Savings and Loan Association, that it may charge him with violation of various securities laws. In a January 24 letter, the SEC staff said it is considering recommending to the commission that it prosecute Mr. Keating, and might seek an order barring him from serving as an officer or director of a public company, said Stephen C. Neal, Mr. Keating's Attorney. Mr. Neal reached at his Chicago home last night, said any SEC actions would be 'basically a waste of taxpayer money'. There are already at least seven state and federal agencies with separate sets of lawyers, regulators and experts pursuing Mr. Keating, he said. The attorney said this message was included in his written response to the SEC, which the commission had demanded by today. In addition, Mr. Neal indicated that 'the SEC letter doesn't shed a clue on what they are looking for. They don't need to pursue litigation for a single day to keep (Mr. Keating) out of public companies and there are already a host of government agencies trying to get all the money he's got, which isn't much.' Mr. Keating has vigorously denied all wrongdoing in connection with the collapse of Lincoln Savings, based in Irvine, Calif." (Reporter, Keating is told by SEC He faces being Charged, 1991)

MICHAEL MILKEN—JUNK-BOND FELONIES

(4) Wall Street Journal Staff Reporter also states, "Washington—Michael and Lowell Milken were formerly barred from the securities industry for life. The junk-bond financier and his brother last year consented to Securities and Exchange Commission proceedings that they won't participate again in the industry that made them both wealthy. The SEC filed the formal administrative order yesterday. The move comes several months after a federal court sentenced Michael Milken, former head of the high-yield bond department at Drexel Burnham Lambert Inc., to 10 years in a California prison after he pleaded to six trading related felonies. Part of Mr. Milken's plea agreement was that the government drop charges against Lowell. The bar from the industry is the standard SEC action in egregious securities law violations. The agency has taken a similar stance in the cases of Ivan Boesky, Dennis

Levine and others. Under terms of the order, the Milkens will be able to reapply for admission at any time, but the agency signaled its unwillingness to accept such a move by not including a time frame for reapplication." (Reporter, Milkens agree to SEC Ban From Securities for Lifetime, March 19,1991)

(4a) Wikipedia puts it that, "Michael Robert Milken (born July 4, 1946) is an American business magnate, financier, and philanthropist noted for his role in the development of the market of high yield bonds also called junk bonds during the 1970s and 1980s, for his 1990 guilty plea to felony charges for violating US securities laws, and for his funding of medical research. Milken was indicted on 98 counts of racketeering and securities fraud in 1989 as a result of an insider trading investigation. After a plea bargain, he pled guilty to six securities and reporting violations but was never convicted of racketeering or insider trading. Milken was sentenced to 10 years in prison and permanently barred from the securities industry by the Securities and Exchange Commission. After the presiding Judge reduced his sentence for cooperating with testimony against his former colleagues and good behavior, he was released after less than two years. Hi critics cited him as the epitome of Wall Street greed during the 1980s, and nicknamed him the 'Junk Bond King.' Supporters, like George Gilder in his book, *Telecosm*, note that 'Milken was a key source of the organizational changes that have impelled economic growth over the last twenty years. Most striking was the productivity surge in capital, as Milken . . . and others took the vast sums trapped in old-line business and put them back into the markets.' . . . Milken's compensation, while head of the high yield bond department at Drexel Burnham Lambert in the late 1980s, exceeded $1 billion in a four year period, a new record for US income at that time. Drexel went bankrupt in 1990. With an estimated net worth of around $2 billion as of 2010, he is ranked by *Forbes* magazine as the 488th richest person in the world. Much of that wealth comes from his success as a bond trader; he only had four losing months in 17 years of trading." (Wikipedia, Michael Milken)

IVAN BOESKY—INSIDER TRADING

(5) According to Wikipedia, "Ivan Frederick Boesky (born March 6, 1937) is an American stock trader who is notable for his prominent role in a Wall Street insider trading scandal that occurred in the United States in the mid-1980s. Boesky was born in Detroit, Michigan, to a Jewish

family. He attended the Cranbrook Kingswood School in Bloomfield Hills before graduating from Detroit's Munford High School. He then took courses at Wayne State University, Eastern Michigan University and the University of Michigan. He was admitted to Detroit College of Law (now Michigan State University College of Law) despite lacking an undergraduate degree and graduated in 1965. In the 1980s, he served as an Adjunct Professor at Columbia University Graduate School of Business and at New York University's Graduate School of Business. By 1986, Boesky had become an arbitrageur who had amassed a fortune of more than US$200 million by betting on corporate takeovers and had also gained control as Chairman of the Beverly Hills Hotel Corp. (after the death of his father-in-law who had run it for 25 years). The U.S. Securities and Exchange Commission investigated him for making investments based on tips received from corporate insiders. These stock acquisitions were sometimes brazen, with massive purchases occurring only a few days before a corporation announced a takeover. Boesky was on the cover of *Time* magazine December 1, 1986. Although insider trading of this kind was illegal, laws prohibiting it were rarely enforced until Boesky was prosecuted. Boesky cooperated with the SEC and informed, including the case against financier Michael Milken. As a result of a plea bargain Boesky received a prison sentence of 3.5 years and was fined $100 million. Although he was released after two years, he was permanently barred from working in securities. He served his sentence at Lompoc Federal Prison Camp near Vandenberg Air Force Base in California. Boesky never recovered his reputation after doing a stint in prison, and paid hundreds of millions of dollars in fines and compensation for his Guinness share-trading fraud role and a number of separate insider dealing scams. Later, he embraced his Judaism and even took classes at the Jewish Theological Seminary of America where he had been a major donor; however, in 1987, following the fallout from his financial scandal, *The New York Times* reported that 'after Ivan F. Boesky had been fined $100 million in the insider trading scandal, the Jewish Theological Seminary, acting at his request, took his name of its $20 million library. His involvement in criminal activities is recounted in the book *Den of Thieves* by James B. Stewart. Another of these events is recounted by Jonathan Guinness in his book 'Requiem for a Family Business' which suggests the SEC granted him immunity from prosecution and allowed to continue to insider trade for significant profit whilst wire-tapping him to entrap others." (Wikipedia C.)

LEHMAN BROTHERS

(6) Wikipedia expresses that, "Lehman Brothers Holdings Inc. (former NYSE ticker symbol LEH) was a global financial services firm. Before declaring bankruptcy in 2008, Lehman was the fourth largest bank in the U.S.A. (behind Goldman Sachs, Morgan Stanley and Merrill Lynch), doing business in investment banking, equity and fixed-income sales and trading (especially U.S. Treasury securities), research, investment management, private equity, and private banking. On September 15, 2008, the firm filed for Chapter 11 bankruptcy protection following the mass exodus of most of its clients, drastic losses in its stock, and devaluation of its assets by credit rating agencies. Lehman Brothers bankruptcy filing is the largest bankruptcy in U.S. history, and is thought to have played a major role in the unfolding of the late 2000's global financial crisis. The following day, Barclays announced its agreement to purchase, subject to regulatory approval, Lehman's North American investment-banking and trading division along with its New York headquarters building. On September 20, 2008, a revised version of that agreement was approved by U.S. Bankruptcy Court Judge James M. Peck. The next week, Nomura Holdings announced that it would acquire Lehman Brothers franchise in the Asia-Pacific region, including Japan, Hong Kong and Australia, as well as Lehman Brothers investment banking and equities business in Europe and the Middle East. The deal became effective on October 13, 2008 . . . . On September 11, 2001, Lehman occupied three floors of One World Trade Center where one of its employees was killed in the terrorist attacks of that day. Its global headquarters in Three World Financial Center were severely damaged and rendered unable by falling debris, displacing over 6,500 employees. The bank recovered quickly and rebuilt its presence. Trading operations moved across the Hudson River to its Jersey City, New Jersey facilities where an impromptu trading floor was built in a Hotel and brought online less than forty-eight hours after the attacks. When Stock Markets reopened in September 17, 2001 Lehman sales and trading capabilities were restored. In the ensuing months, the firm fanned out its operations across the New York City metropolitan area in over 40 temporary locations. Notably, the investment-banking division converted the first floor lounges, restaurants and all the 665 guestrooms of the Sheraton Manhattan Hotel into office space. The bank also experimented with flex-time (to share office space) and telecommuting via virtual private networking. In October 2001, Lehman purchased a 32 storey,

1,050,000-square-foot office building for a reported sum of $700 million. The building located at 745 Seventh Avenue, had recently been completed, and not yet occupied, by rival Morgan Stanley.... The firm was criticized for not moving back to its former headquarters in lower Manhattan. Following the attacks, only Deutsche Bank, Goldman Sachs, and Merrill Lynch, of the major firms, remained in the downtown area. Lehman, however, points to the facts that it was committed to stay in New York, that the new headquarters represented an ideal circumstance where the firm was desperate to buy and Morgan Stanley was desperate to sell, that when the new building was purchased, the structural integrity of Three World Financial Center had not yet been given a clean bill of health, and that in any case, the company could not have waited until May 2002 for repairs to Three World Financial Center to conclude.... In 2003, the company was one of ten firms which simultaneously entered into a settlement with the U.S. Securities and Exchange Commission (SEC), the office of the New York State Attorney General and various other securities regulators, regarding undue influence over each firm's research analysts by its investment-banking divisions. Specifically, regulators alleged that the firms had improperly associated analyst compensation with the firm's investment-banking revenues, and promised favorable market-moving research coverage, in exchange for underwriting opportunities. The settlement known as the 'global settlement' provided for the total financial penalties of $1.4 billion, including $80 million against Lehman, and structural reforms, including a complete separation of investment banking departments from research departments, no analyst compensation, directly or indirectly, from investment banking-revenues, and the provision of free, independent, third party, research to the firm's clients.... A March 2010 report by the court-appointed examiner indicated that Lehman executives regularly used cosmetic accounting gimmicks at the end of each quarter to make its finances appear less shaky than they really were. This practice was a type of repurchase agreement that temporarily removed securities form the company's balance sheet. However, unlike typical repurchase agreements, these deals were described by Lehman as the outright sale of securities and created 'a materially misleading picture of the firm's financial condition in the late 2007 and 2008. In August 2007, the firm closed its subprime lender, BNC Mortgage, eliminating 1,200 positions in 23 locations, and took an after tax charge of $25 million and a $27 million reduction in goodwill. Lehman said that poor market conditions in the mortgage space 'necessitated a substantial reduction in the resources and capacity in the subprime space'. In 2008, Lehman faced an unprecedented loss to the continuing subprime mortgage crisis. Lehman's loss was a result of having held on to large portions in subprime and other lower-rated mortgage tranches when securing the underlying mortgages; whether Lehman did this because it was simply unable to sell the lower-rated bonds, or make a conscious decision to hold them, is unclear in any event, huge losses accrued in lower-rated mortgage-backed securities throughout2008. In the second fiscal quarter, Lehman reported losses of $2.8 billion and was forced to sell off $6 billion in assets. In the first half of 2008 alone, Lehman lost 73% of its value as the credit market continued to tighten. In August 2008, Lehman reported that it intended to release 6% of its work force, 1,500 people, just ahead of its third-quarter-reporting deadline in September . . . . Investor confidence continued to erode as Lehman stock lost roughly half its value and pushed the S&P 500 down 3.4 % on September 9. The Dow Jones lost 300 points the same day on investors' concerns about the security of the bank. The U.S. Government did not announce any plans to assist with any possible financial crisis that emerged at Lehman. The next day, Lehman announced a loss of $3.9 billion and its intent to sell off a majority stake in its investment-management business, which includes Neuberger Berman. The stock slid 7% that day. Lehman after earlier rejecting questions on the sale of the company, was reportedly searching for a buyer as its stock price dropped another 40% on September 11, 2008. Just before the collapse of Lehman Brothers, executives of Neuberger Berman sent email memos suggesting, among other things, that the Lehman Brothers top people forego multimillion dollar bonuses to 'send a strong message to both employees and investors that management is not shirking accountability for recent performance' . . . . Shortly before 1 a.m. Monday morning (New York time), Lehman Brothers Holdings announced it would file for Chapter 11 bankruptcy protection citing bank debt of $613 billion, $155 billion in bond debt, and assets worth $639 billion. It further announced that its subsidiaries would continue to operate as normal. A group of Wall Street firms agreed to provide capital and financial assistance for the bank's orderly liquidation and the Federal Reserve, in turn, agreed to a swap of lower quality-assets in exchange for loans and other assistance from the government. The morning witnessed scenes of Lehman employees removing files, items with the company logo, and other belongings from the world headquarters at 745 Seventh Avenue. The spectacle continued throughout the day and into the following day . . . .

On March 11, 2010, Antan R. Valukas, a court appointed examiner, published the results of its year-long investigation into the finances of Lehman Brothers. This report revealed that Lehman Brothers used accounting procedure termed repo 105 to temporarily exchange $50 billion of assets into cash just before publishing its financial statements. The action could be seen to implicate both, Ernst & Young, the bank's accounting firm and Richard S. Fuld Jr., the former CEO. This could potentially lead to Ernst & Young being found guilty of financial malpractice and Fuld facing time in prison. According to the Wall Street Journal, in March 2011, the SEC announced that they weren't confident that they could prove that Lehman Brothers violated U.S. Laws in its accounting practices. In October 2011, the administrators of Lehman Brothers Holding Inc. lost their appeal to overturn a court order forcing them to pay 148 million pounds into their underfunded pensions plan." (Wikipedia, Lehman Brothers)

BERNARD MADOFF—PONZI SCHEME

(7) Wikipedia points out that, "The Madoff Investment Scandal broke in December 2008 when former NASDAQ chairman Bernard Madoff admitted that the wealth management arm of his business was an elaborate Ponzi scheme. [Some sources on Wall Street claimed that Bernard Madoff under the auspices of the NASDAQ had bought out the American Stock Exchange, only to relinquish it, as it was going into a tailspin, and dying a painful cancerous death. It is difficult to believe that Bernie did not make anything off the American Stock Exchange deal along with his appointed executives, and the truth to this episode may yet have to be discovered and investigated by the SEC with possible prosecution.] Madoff founded the Wall Street firm Bernard L Madoff Investment Securities LLC in 1960, and was its chairman until his arrest. Alerted by his sons, federal authorities arrested Madoff on December 11, 2008. On March 12, 2009, Madoff pled guilty to 11 federal crimes and admitted to operating what has been the Ponzi scheme in history. On June 29, 2009, he was sentenced to 150 years in prison with restitution of $170 billion. According to the original federal charges, Madoff said that his firm had 'liabilities of approximately U.S. $50 billion.' Prosecutors estimated the size of the fraud to be $64 billion, based on the amounts in the accounts of Madoff's 4,800 clients as of November 30, 2008. Ignoring opportunity costs and taxes paid on fictitious profits, half of Madoff's direct investors lost no money. Investors have determined others were

involved in the scheme. The U.S. Securities and Exchange Commission (SEC) has also come under fire for not investigating Madoff more thoroughly; questions about his firm has been raised as early as 1999. Madoff's business, in the process of liquidation, was one of the top market makers on Wall Street and in 2008, the sixth largest. Madoff's personal and business asset freeze has created a chain reaction throughout the worlds business and philanthropic community, facing many organizations to at least temporarily close, including the Robert I. Lappin Charitable Foundation, the Picower Foundation, and the JEHT Foundation. Madoff started his firm in 1960 as a penny stock trader with $5,000 (about $35,000 in 2008) earned from working as a lifeguard and sprinkler installer. His fledging business began to grow with the assistance of his father-in-law, accountant Saul Alpern, who referred a circle of friends and their families. Initially the firm made markets (quoted bid and ask prices) via the National Quotation Bureau's Pink Sheets. In order to compete with firms that were members of the New York Stock Exchange, trading on the stock exchange's floor, his firm began using innovative computer information technology to disseminate its quotes. After a trial run, the technology that the firm helped develop became the NASDAQ. At one point, Madoff's Securities was the largest buying and selling 'market maker' at the NASDAQ. He was active in the National Association of Securities Dealers (NASD), a self-regulatory securities industry organization, serving as the Chairman of the Board of Directors and on the Board of Governors. In 1992, The Wall Street Journal described him 'one of the masters of the off-exchange third market' and the bane of the New York Stock Exchange. He has built a highly profitable securities firm, Bernard L. Madoff Investment Securities, which siphons a huge volume of stock trades away from the Big Board. The $740 million average daily volume of trades executed electronically by the Madoff firm off the exchange equals 9% of the New York Exchange's. Mr. Madoff's firm can execute trades so quickly and cheaply that it actually pays other brokerage firms a penny a share to execute their customers' orders, profiting from the spread between bids and ask prices that most stocks trade for . . . . Federal Investigators believe the fraud in the investment management division and advisory division may have begun in the 1970s. However, Madoff himself stated his fraudulent activities began in the 1990s. In the 1980s, Madoff's market-maker division trade up to 5% of the total volume made on the New York Stock Exchange. Madoff was the first prominent practitioner who paid a broker to execute a customer's order through his brokerage called 'legal kickback' which gave Madoff the reputation of being the largest dealer in NYSE-listed stocks in the U.S., trading about 15% of transaction volume. Academics have questioned the ethics of these payments. Madoff has argued that these payments did not alter the price that the customer received. He viewed the payments as a normal business practice. 'If your girlfriend goes to buy stockings at a supermarket, the rack that display those stockings are usually paid for by the company that manufactured the stockings. Order flow is an issued that attracted a lot of attention but is grossly overrated.' By 2000, Madoff Securities, one of the top traders of U.S. securities, held approximately $300 million in assets. The business occupied three floors of the Lipstick Building, with the investment management division, referred to as the 'hedge fund', employing a staff of approximately 24. Madoff ran a branch of the office in London, separate from Madoff Securities, which employed 28, handling investments for his family of approximately 80 million pounds sterling. Two remote cameras installed in the London office permitted Madoff to monitor events from New York. . . . Purported Strategy—Madoff's sale pitch was an investment strategy consisting of purchasing blue-chip stocks and taking options contracts on them, sometimes called a split-strike conversion or a collar. Typically, a position will consist of the ownership of 30-35 S&P 100 stocks, most correlated to that index, the sale of out-of-the-money 'calls' on the index, and the purchase of the out-of-the-money 'puts' on the index. The sale of the 'call' is designed to increase the rate of return, while allowing upward movement of the stock portfolio to the strike of the 'calls'. The 'puts' funded in large part by the sales of the 'calls', limit the portfolio's downside.' [This ought to have raised a red-flag about options trades on the AMEX, by Bernie Madoff or his company before and after he bought over the AMEX. Whatever happened to the Stock Watch Department of the American Stock Exchange? Not to mention that the U.S. Securities and Exchange Commission may have fallen asleep at the wheel, by not investigating the purchase and takeover/merger by Madoff's company—the NASD, of the American Stock Exchange. The first reason being, that with Madoff's boasting of his options trading strategy, it surely should have raised some sort of red-flag on options trading volumes and activity; especially since he was expressing an interest in owning the AMEX. The American Stock Exchange was the largest Options Exchange on the East Coast, and second largest to the "Chicago Board of Options Exchange," on the West Coast of the United States. After Madoff bought out the AMEX, the argument could have been made that with him at the helm and his appointed executives in charge of the AMEX; who would scrutinized the entire joint operation?] In 1992, 'Avillino and Bienes' interview with The Wall Street Journal, Madoff discussed his supposed methods. In the 1970s he had placed invested funds in 'convertible arbitrage positions in large-capped stocks, with promised investment returns of 18% to 20%,' and in 1982, he began using futures contracts on the stock index, and then placed put options on futures during the 1987 stock market crash. A few analysts performing due diligence had been unable to replicate the Madoff funds past returns using historic price data for U.S. stocks and options on the indices. *Barron's* raised the possibility that Madoff's returns were most likely due to front running his firm's brokerage clients . . . . In his guilty plea, Madoff admitted that he hadn't actually traded since the mid 1990's and all of his returns since he has been fabricated. However, David Scheehan, principal investigator for Picard, believes the wealth management arm of Madoff's business had always been fraudulent. Madoff's operation differed form a typical Ponzi scheme. While most Ponzis were based on nonexistent businesses, Madoff's brokerage operation was very real . . . . Madoff was a 'master marketer,' and his fund was considered exclusive, giving an appearance of a 'velvet rope.' He generally refused to meet directly with investors, which gave him an 'Oz' aura and increased the allure of the investment. Some Madoff investors were weary of removing their money from his fund, in case they could not get back in later . . . . The Swiss Bank, Union Bancaire Privee, explained that because of Madoff's huge volume as broker-dealer, the bank believed he had a perceived edge on the market because his trades were timed well, suggesting they believe he was front-running. Access to Washington—The Madoff family gained unusual access to Washington's lawmakers and regulators through the industry's top trade group. The Madoff family has long-standing, high-level ties to the Securities Industry and Financial Markets Association (SIFMA), the primary securities industry organization. Bernard Madoff sat on the Board of Directors of the Securities Industry Association, which merged with the Bond Market Association in 2006 to form SIFMA . . . . Madoff Securities LLC was investigated at least eight times over a 16 year period by the U.S. Securities and Exchange Commission (SEC) and other regulatory authorities . . . . The SEC investigation came right in the middle of Madoff's three terms as the chairman of the NASD stock market board . . . . The SEC investigated Madoff in 1999 and 2000 about concerns that the firm was hiding customers' orders from other traders, for which Madoff then took corrective measures. In 2001, an SEC official met with Harry Markopolos at their Boston regional office and reviewed his allegations of Madoff's fraudulent practices. The SEC claimed it conducted two other enquiries into Madoff in the last several years, but did not find any violations or major issues of concern. In 2004, after published articles appeared accusing the firm of front-running, the SEC's Washington office cleared Madoff. The SEC detailed that inspectors had examined Madoff's brokerage operation in 2005, checking for three kinds of violations: the strategy he used for customer accounts, the requirement of brokers to obtain the best possible price for customer orders, and operating as an unregistered investment advisor. Madoff was registered as a broker-dealer, but doing business as an asset manager. 'The staff found no evidence of fraud.' In September 2005, Madoff agreed to register his business, but the SEC kept its findings confidential. During the 2005 investigation, Meaghan Cheung, a branch head of the SEC's New York's Enforcement Division, was the person responsible for the oversight and blunder, according Harry Markopolos, who testified on February 4, 2009, at a hearing held by a House Financial Services Subcommittee on Capital Markets. In 2007, SEC enforcement completed an investigation which began on January 6, 2006, into a Ponzi scheme allegation which resulted in neither a finding of fraud, nor referral to the SEC Commissioners for legal action.... Investigators are looking for others involved in the scheme, despite Madoff's assertion that he alone was responsible for the large scale operation. Harry Susman, an attorney representing several clients of the firm, stated that 'someone had to create the appearance that there were returns' and further suggested that there must have been a team buying and selling stocks, forging books, and filing reports. James Ratley, president of the Association of Certified Fraud Examiners said, 'In order for him to have done this by himself, he would have had to have been at work night and day, no vacation and no time off. He would have had to nurture the Ponzi scheme daily. What happened when he was gone? Who handled it when somebody called in while he was on vacation and said 'I need access to money'? Simply from an administrative perspective, the act of putting together the various account statements, which did show trading activity, has to involve a number of people. You would need office and support personnel, people who actually knew what the market prices were for the securities that were being traded. You would need accountants so that the internal documents reconcile with the documents being sent to customers at least on a superficial basis,' said Tom Dewey, a securities lawyer . . . . [Several individuals including Madoff's two sons Mark and Andrew were found to have had an intricate knowledge of and complicity in Bernard Madoff's elaborate Ponzi scheme.] The original criminal complaint estimated that investors lost $50 billion through the scheme, though *The Wall Street Journal* reports, that figure includes the alleged false profits that Madoff's firm reported to its customers for decades. It is unclear exactly how much investors deposited into the firm. He was originally charged with a single count of securities fraud and faced up to 20 years in prison, and a fine of $55 million if convicted. Court papers indicate that Madoff's firm had about 4,800 investment client accounts as of November 30, 2008, and issued statements for that month reporting that client accounts held a total balance of about $65 billion, but actually 'held only a small fraction' of that balance for clients. Madoff was arrested by Federal Bureau of Investigation (FBI) on December 11, 2008, on a criminal charge of securities fraud. According to the criminal complaint, the previous day he had told his sons that his business was 'a giant Ponzi scheme'. They called a friend for advice, Martin Flumenbaum, a lawyer, who called federal prosecutors and the SEC on their behalf. FBI Agent Theodore Cacioppi made a house call. 'We are here to find out if there is an innocent explanation,' Cacioppi said quietly. The 70 year old financier paused, and then said 'There is no innocent explanation.' He had 'paid investors with money that was not there'. Madoff was released on the same day of his arrest after posting $10 million bail. Madoff and his wife surrendered their passports, and he was subject to travel restrictions, a 7 p.m. curfew at his co-op, and electronic monitoring as a condition of bail. Although Madoff only had two co-signers for his $10 million bail, his wife and his brother Peter, rather than the four required, a judge allowed him free on bail but ordered him confined to his apartment. Madoff has reportedly received death threats that have been referred to the FBI, and the SEC referred to fears of 'harm or flight' in its request for Madoff to be confined to his Upper East Side Apartment. Cameras monitored his apartment's doors, its communication devices sent signals to the FBI, and his wife was required to pay for additional security. Apart from 'Bernard I. Madoff' and 'Bernard I. Madoff Investment Securities L.L.C. (BMIS)', the order to freeze all activities also forbade trading from the companies Madoff Securities International Ltd. ('Madoff International') and Madoff Ltd. On January 5, 2009, prosecutors had requested that the Court revoke his bail, after Madoff and his wife allegedly violated the court-ordered asset freeze by mailing jewelry worth up to $1 million to relatives, including their sons and Madoff's brother. It was also noted that $173 million in signed checks had been found in Madoff's office desk after he had been arrested. His sons reported the mailings to prosecutors. Previously, Madoff was thought to be cooperating with prosecutors. The following week, Judge Ellis refused the government's request to revoke Madoff's bail, but required as a condition of bail that Madoff make an inventory of personal items and that his mail be searched. On March 10, 2009, the United States Attorney for the Southern District of New York filed an 11-count criminal information or complaint charging Madoff with 11 federal crimes: securities fraud, investment advisor fraud, mail fraud, wire fraud, three counts of money laundering, false statements, perjury, making false filings with the SEC, and theft from an employee benefit plan. The complaint stated that Madoff had defrauded his clients of almost $65 billion—thus spelling out the largest Ponzi scheme in history, as well as the largest investor fraud committed by a single person. Madoff pleaded guilty to three counts of money laundering. Prosecutors allege that he used the London Office, Madoff Securities International Ltd. To launder more than $250 million of client money by transferring client money from the investment—advisory business in New York to London and then back to the U.S. to support the U.S. trading operation of Bernard I. Madoff Investment Securities L.L.C. Madoff gave the appearance that he was trading in Europe for his clients. Plea Proceedings: On March 12, 2009, Madoff appeared in court in a plea proceeding, and pleaded guilty of all charges. There was no plea agreement between the government and Madoff, he simply pleaded guilty and signed a waiver of indictment. The charges carried a maximum sentence of 150 years in prison, as well as mandatory restitution and fines up to twice the gross gain or loss derived from the offenses. If the government's estimate is correct, Madoff will have to pay $7.2 billion in restitution. In his pleading allocution, Madoff admitted to running a Ponzi scheme and expressed regret for his 'criminal acts'. He stated that he had begun his scheme sometime in the early 1990's. He wished to satisfy his clients' expectations of high returns he had promised, even though it was during an economic recession. He admitted that he hadn't invested any of his clients' money since the inception of the scheme. Instead, he merely deposited the money into his business account at Chase Manhattan Bank. He admitted to false trading activities masked by foreign transfers and false SEC returns. When clients requested account withdrawals, he paid them from the Chase account, claiming the profits were the result of his own unique 'split-strike conversion strategy'. He said he had every intention of terminating the scheme, but it proved 'difficult, and ultimately impossible' to extricate himself. He eventually reconciled himself to being exposed as a fraud. Only two of at least 25 victims who had requested to be heard at the hearing spoke in the open court against accepting Madoff's plea of guilt. Judge Denny Chin accepted his guilty plea and remanded him to incarceration at the Manhattan Metropolitan Correctional Center until sentencing. Chin said that Madoff was now a substantial flight risk given his age, wealth and possibility of spending the rest of his life in prison . . . . Madoff was incarcerated at Butner Federal Correctional Complex outside Raleigh, North Carolina. His inmate number is #61727-054. On July 28, 2009, he gave his first jailhouse interview to Joseph Cotchett and Nancy Fineman, attorneys from San Francisco, because they threatened to sue his wife, Ruth, on behalf of several investors who lost fortunes. During the 4 and ½ hour session, he was described as arrogant and cocky, and upon query, apologized to all his clients. Recovery of Funds: . . . Madoff's combined assets are about $826 million and have been frozen. Madoff provided a confidential list of his and his firm's assets to the SEC on December 31, which was subsequently disclosed on March 13, 2009 in a court filing. Madoff had no IRAs, no 401(k), no Keogh plan, no other pension plan and no annuities. He owned less than a combined $200,000 in securities in Lehman Brothers, Morgan Stanley, Fidelity, Bear Sterns, and M&T. No offshore or Swiss Bank Accounts were listed. On March 17, 2009, prosecutor filed a document listing more assets including $2.6 million in jewelry and about 35 sets of watches and cufflinks, more than $30 million in loans owed to the couple by their sons, and Ruth Madoff's interest in real estate funds sponsored by Sterling Equities, whose partners include Fred Wilpon. Ruth Madoff, and Peter Madoff, invested as 'passive limited partners' in real estate funds sponsored by the company, as well as other venture investments. Assets also include the Madoff's interest in Hoboken Radiology LLC, in Hoboken, New Jersey, Delivery Concepts LLC, an online food ordering service in midtown Manhattan that operates as 'delivery.com' an interest in Madoff La Brea LLC, an interest in the restaurant, PJ Clarke's on the Hudson LLC, and Boca Raton, Florida based Viager II LLC. On March2, 2009, Judge Lewis Stanton modified an existing freeze order to surrender assets Madoff owns: his securities firm, real estate, artwork, and entertainment tickets, and granted a request by prosecutors that the existing freeze remain in place for the Manhattan apartment, and vacation homes in Montauk, New York, and Palm Beach, Florida. He has also agreed to surrender his interest in Primex Holdings LLC, a joint venture between Madoff Securities and several large brokerages, designed to replicate the auction process on the New York Stock Exchange. Madoff's April14, 2009 opening day New York Mets tickets were sold for $7,500 on EBay." (Wikipedia, Madoff Investment Scandal)

ALLEN STANFORD—PONZI SCHEME

(8) Wikipedia notes that, "Allen Stanford (born March 24, 1950) is a former prominent financier and sponsor of professional sports who is in prison serving a 110 year sentence having been convicted of charges that his investment company was a massive Ponzi scheme and fraud. Stanford was the chairman of the now defunct Stanford Financial Group of companies. A fifth generation Texan who once resided in Saint Croix, U.S. Virgin Islands, he holds dual citizenship, being a citizen of Antigua and Barbuda and the United States. In early 2009, Stanford became the subject of several fraud investigations, and on February 17, 2009, was charged by the U.S. Securities and Exchange Commission (SEC) with fraud and multiple violations of U.S. Securities laws for alleged 'massive ongoing fraud' involving $7 billion in certificates of deposits. The Federal Bureau of Investigation (FBI) raided Stanford's offices in Houston, Texas; Memphis, Tennessee, and Tupelo, Mississippi. On February 27, 2009 the SEC amended its complaint to describe the alleged fraud as a 'massive Ponzi scheme'. He 'voluntarily surrendered' to authorities on June 18, 2009. On March 6, 2012, Stanford was convicted on all charges except a single count of wire fraud. Stanford grew up in Mexia, Texas. His father, James Stanford is a former Mayor of Mexia, and a member of the Board of Directors of Stanford Financial Group. His mother, Sammie, is a nurse. After his parents divorced in 1959, Stanford and his brother went to live with their mother. Both of his parents remarried. Stanford started in business in Waco, Texas, opening a bodybuilding gym that failed. His first success in business came from speculating in real estate in Houston after the Texan oil bubble burst in the early 1980s; his partner in this venture was his father, James: the two men made a fortune in the 1980s, buying up depressed real estate and selling it years later as the market recovered. After his father retired in 1993, Stanford took control of a company with 500 employees. Reports surfaced early in February 2009 that the SEC, the FBI, the Florida

Office of Financial Regulation, and the Financial Industry Regulatory Authority (FINRA), a major U.S. private-sector oversight body, were investigating Stanford's company Stanford Financial Group, questioning the consistently higher-than-market returns which Stanford International Bank claimed to make for its depositors. A former executive told SEC officials that Stanford presented hypothetical investment results as actual historical data in sales pitches to clients. Stanford claimed his CDs were as safe as, or safer than, U.S. Government insured accounts. [How could anyone as an investor be so gullible as to believe that? Naturally, greed on the side of investors blinded them and took away their reasoning power. Investors, anything that seem too good to be true is most likely so. His CDs could not have been safer than those of the U.S. Government insured accounts—unless his CDs were insured by some higher power or authority]. A leaked cable from the U.S. Embassy in the Bahamas reported as early as 2006 that companies under Stanford's control were 'rumored to engage in bribery, money laundering, and political manipulation'. The U.S. Ambassador to the Bahamas at the time was reported to have 'managed to stay out of any one-on-one photos with Stanford' during a charity breakfast event. Federal agents raided the offices of Stanford on February 17, 2009, and treated it as 'a kind of crime scene—cautioning people not to leave fingerprints. The SEC charged Allen Stanford with 'massive ongoing fraud' centered on an $8 billion investment scheme. Stanford's assets, along with those of his companies, were frozen and placed into receivership by a U.S. Federal Judge, who also ordered Stanford to surrender his passport. CNBC later reported that Stanford tried to flee the country on the same day as the raid on his headquarters: he contact a private jet owner and attempted to pay for a flight to Antigua with a credit card, but was refused because the company would accept only a 'wire transfer'. FBI agents, acting at the request of the SEC, on February 19, located Stanford at his girlfriend's house near Fredericksburg, Virginia, and served him with civil legal papers filed by the SEC. Stanford was not arrested until June 18, 2009. Stanford surrendered his passport to federal prosecutors, and hired criminal defense lawyer Brendan Sullivan, known for having represented Oliver North. The SEC often files civil charges before criminal charges are filed . . . . On February 27, 2009, the SEC said that Stanford and his accomplices operated a 'massive Ponzi scheme', misappropriated billions of dollars of investors' money and falsified the Stanford International Bank's records to hide their fraud. 'Stanford International Bank's financial statements, including its investment income, are fictional' the SEC said. In an interview on April 20 at the law offices of Houston criminal attorney Dick DeGuerin, however, Stanford denied any wrongdoing. His companies had been well-run, he claimed, until the SEC 'disemboweled' them. On June 18, 2009, Stanford was taken into custody by FBI agents. According to DeGuerin: Federal agents in black SUVs surrounded his girlfriend's house this afternoon, and just sat there. I told him to walk out and introduce himself. So he did, and asked them, 'If you've got a warrant, take me into custody. If you don't, I'm going to Houston. And they did, so they arrested him. [This man certainly had some nerve. Men in this investment business tend to use the "cost-benefit-analysis calculus"; since anyone caught in this type of "white-collar-crime" usually neither admit nor deny what they have been charged with: and given a slap on the wrist with a few million dollars in fine, after they have robbed investors of billions of dollars, or barred from ever trading in the industry for life. This was one of those times when Stanford like a few others miscalculated a long prison term.] On June 25, 2009, Stanford appeared in a Houston court and pleaded not guilty to charges of fraud, conspiracy and obstruction. His lawyer claimed that Stanford had resorted to liberal alcohol intake to grapple with the strain of the proceedings. On August 27, 2009, Stanford was admitted into the Conroe, Texas Regional Medical Center. He was being transported from the private prison in Huntsville, Texas to the Federal Courthouse in Houston to attend a hearing concerning his attorney, who had asked the court to be dismissed from Stanford's case. En route, Stanford complained of a racing heart. On September 26, 2009, Stanford was hospitalized due to injuries sustained in a fight with another inmate at the private Joe Corley Detention Facility. His injuries were described as non-life threatening. Stanford's trial date was set for January 2011, but this was delayed due to his poor health. Stanford's Federal Bureau of Prisons # 35017-183, is incarcerated at the Federal Detention Center, Houston. In February 2011, Stanford issued a counter-claim of $7.2 billion of damages against the FBI and the SEC. In May prosecutors dropped seven charges against Stanford, leaving 14 charges ongoing. By November 5, 2011, Stanford was being held at the Federal Medical Center, Butner, North Carolina, as part of the Butner Federal Correctional Complex. Stanford's attorneys claimed that their client was unfit to stand trial due to amnesia resulting from his sustained injuries. On December 22, 2011, however, he was found competent to stand trial by a U.S. District Judge. On January 24, 2012, Stanford entered the Houston Federal

Courthouse, U.S. District Judge David Hittner presiding, and the trial began. He was convicted by a jury as the leader of the Ponzi scheme worth $7 billion on March 6, 2012. On June 14, 2012, Stanford was sentenced to 110 years in prison for cheating investors out of more than $7 billion over 20 years in one of the largest Ponzi schemes in U.S. history." (Wikipedia, Allen Stanford, 2012)

WELLS FARGO BANK—RIGGING OF TRANSACTIONS

(9) In the words of Brent Kendall, "Washington—Wells Fargo & Co. has agreed to pay $148 million to settle charges that its Wachovia Bank unit participated in a conspiracy that rigged bids on investment contracts for municipalities, federal and state authorities said. The agreement is the latest enforcement action in a long running U.S. investigation into the municipal-securities market. Wachovia is the fourth bank to reach a settlement. The Justice Department, Securities and Exchange Commission and state authorities said former Wachovia employees, working in conjunction with others rigged the bidding process for government entities that were seeking to invest money raised through municipal bonds. The SEC said Wachovia rigged at least 58 transactions in 25 states and Puerto Rico. Wachovia's conduct took place from at least 1997 to 2005, the agency said, before it was acquired by Wells Fargo during the heat of the 2008 financial crisis. Wells Fargo said it fully cooperated in the investigation and was pleased to resolve the matter. 'Wells Fargo does not endorse, ratify or condone anticompetitive activity or other violations of law,' the bank said." [There ought to be serious scrutiny and better regulations of America's banks that caused the financial crisis that the nation experienced. However, having new regulations can only be effective if there are ample resources to deal with the infractions. The Treasury Department should stop favoring banks in preference to homeowners and investors, as was done with TARP]. (Kendall, December 9, 2011)

PHILIP FALCONE—FRAUD CHARGES

(10) Steve Eder and Jean Eaglesham writes, "Prominent hedge-fund manage Philip Falcone has rejected a Securities and Exchange Commission settlement offer that would have banned him from the securities industry and essentially ended his career, people familiar with the matter said. The move by SEC Officials to reach a settlement came before an affiliate of Mr.

Falcone's firm, Harbinger Capital Partners LLC, disclosed in a securities filing Dec. 9 that he and two senior executives have been warned by the SEC they could face civil fraud charges. An SEC spokesman declined to comment. A Harbinger spokesman said 'any comment on settlement talks would be inappropriate.' The SEC's push for a multi-year ban on the 49-year-old billionaire from the hedge-fund industry is a sign of how seriously agency officials view alleged misconduct by Mr. Falcone that is now being investigated, people familiar with the matter said. Mr. Falcone rose to prominence in 2007 with lucrative bets against subprime mortgages, and he is known for both big gains and big losses. The SEC is scrutinizing his hedge-fund business on three fronts, according to regulatory filings. In March, Harbinger said it was under investigation by the SEC for possible market manipulation. The agency also said it was probing a loan Mr. Falcone took out from the fund in October 2009. In the firm's regulatory filing earlier this month, Harbinger disclosed an unspecified third issue related to agreements with certain investors. The Wall Street Journal has reported that the third matter is tied to whether Harbinger improperly agreed to allow some investors, including Goldman Sachs Group Inc., to cash out of their holdings, while barring other clients from withdrawing their money, according to people familiar with the matter. An SEC multi-year ban likely would make it impossible for Mr. Falcone to continue running his hedge-fund as a hands on operation. Such a ban likely would include barring him from managing assets of the investors in his fund, people familiar with the matter said. If Mr. Falcone agreed to an exile, it also would threaten his bet on LightSquared Inc., a new wireless communications firm. Mr. Falcone is trying to win crucial regulatory approval for LightSquared but faces resistance from some lawmakers, including Sen. Charles Grassley (R., Iowa). [Here is another example of a big money lobbyist at work with a member of Congress.] In a letter to Mr. Grassley in July, the chairman of the Federal Communications Commission, which will decide on granting crucial broadcasting spectrum allocations to LightSquared, said it had a 'character policy' that is part of licensing decisions. The regulator 'will consider certain forms of non FCC related misconduct,' the letter said. The letter noted that the FCC usually doesn't consider allegations that haven't resulted in a conviction. An FCC spokesman couldn't be reached for comment Thursday. Mr. Falcone and Harbinger haven't been charged. The SEC's determination to push Mr. Falcone at least temporarily out of the business where he made his name and fortune comes amid pressure on the agency from lawmakers to show it takes a tough enforcement stance. 'The SEC has a varied but limited number of sanctions, and it's certainly under pressure to be drawing on its entire arsenal, and that includes industry bans as well as monetary penalties,' said Daniel Richman, a law professor at Columbia University. Bans have part of some civil fraud settlements reached by the SEC recently. In September, Barr Rosenberg, the co-founder of Investment Management firm AXA Rosenberg Group LLC, agreed to a lifetime bar from working in the securities industry. The SEC accused Mr. Rosenberg of concealing an error in the computer code of the investment model his firm used to manage client assets. Mr. Rosenberg didn't admit or deny wrongdoing. Harbinger's assets hit $26 billion in 2008 as investors flocked to the fund, but setbacks since then include investment losses and client withdrawals. In the third quarter, Harbinger's assets fell to less than $5 billion, according to investor documents. LightSquared has been beset by technical challenges and accusations of trying to improperly influence regulators. The company has denied any wrongdoing." (Eaglesham S. E., Friday, December 23, 2011)

AMERICAN INTERNATIONAL GROUP—(AIG)

(11) Wikipedia claims that, "AIG is an American multinational insurance corporation. Its corporate headquarters is reported as 180 Maiden Lane, in New York City (and was formerly in the American International Building in New York City). The British headquarters office is on Fenchurch Street in London, continental Europe operations are based in La Defense, Paris, and its Asian headquarters office is in Hong Kong. According to the 2011 Forbes Global 2000 list, AIG was the 29th largest public company in the world. It was listed on the Dow Jones Industrial Average from April 8, 2004 t0 September 22, 2008. AIG suffered from a liquidity crisis when its credit ratings were downgraded below 'AA' levels in September 2008. The United States Federal Reserve Bank on September 16, 2008 created an $85 billion credit facility to enable the company to meet increased collateral obligations consequent to the credit rating downgrade, in exchange for the issuance of a stock warrant to the Federal Reserve Bank for 79.9% of the equity of AIG. The Federal Reserve Bank and the United States Treasury by May 2009 had increased the potential financial support to AIG, with the support of an investment of as much as $70 billion, a $60 billion credit line and $52.5 billion to buy mortgage-based assets owned or guaranteed by AIG, increasing the total among available to as much as $182.5 billion. AIG subsequently

sold a number of its subsidiaries and other assets, to off down loans received, and continues to seek buyers of its assets. Beginning in 2005, AIG became embroiled in a series of fraud investigations conducted by the Securities and Exchange Commission, U.S. Justice Department, and New York State Attorney General's Office. Greenberg was ousted amid an accounting scandal in February 2005; he is still fighting civil charges being pursued by New York State. The New York Attorney General's investigation led to a $1.6 billion fine for AIG and criminal charges for some of its executives. Greenberg was succeeded as CEO by Martin J. Sullivan, who had begun his career at AIG as a clerk in its London Office in 1970. AIG purchased the remaining 39% that it did not own of online auto insurance specialist 21st Century Insurance in 2007 for $749 million. With the failure of the parent company and the continuing recession in the late 2008, AIG rebranded its insurance unit to 21st Century Insurance. On June 15, 2008, after disclosure of financial losses and subsequent to a falling stock price, Sullivan resigned and was replaced by Robert B. Willumstad, Chairman of the AIG Board of Directors since 2006. Willumstad was forced by the U.S. Government to step down and was replaced by Edward M. Liddy on September 17, 2008. AIG's board of directors named Robert Benmosche CEO on August 3, 2009 to replace Mr. Liddy, who earlier in the year announced his retirement.... On the evening of September 16, 2008, the Federal Reserve Bank's Board of Governors announced that the Federal Reserve Bank of New York had been authorized to create a 24-month credit-liquidity facility from which AIG could draw up to $85 billion. The loan was collateralized by the assets of AIG, the three-month London Interbank Offered Rate (LIBOR) (i.e. LIBOR plus 8.5%).... [See LIBOR, as explained in chapter three that shows LIBOR to be the worst and largest Wall Street scandal ever.] Maurice Greenberg, former CEO of AIG, on September 17, 2008, characterized the bailout as a nationalization of AIG. He also stated that he was bewildered by the situation and was at a loss over how the entire situation got out of control as it did. On September 17, 2008, Federal Reserve Board chair Ben Bernanke asked Treasury Secretary Henry Paulson join him, to call on members of Congress, to describe the need for a congressionally authorized bailout of the nation's banking system. Weeks later, Congress approved the Emergency Economic Stabilization Act of 2008. Bernanke said to Paulson on September 17, 'We can't keep doing this. Both because we at the Fed don't have the necessary resources and for reasons of democratic legitimacy, it's important that the Congress come in and takes control of the situation'.... In March 2009, AIG announced that they were paying $165 million in executive bonuses. Total bonuses for the financial unit could reach $450 million and bonuses for the entire company could reach $1.2 billion. President Barack Obama, who voted for the AIG bailout as a Senator responded to the planned payments by saying 'It's hard to understand how derivative traders at AIG warranted any bonuses much less $165 million in extra pay. How do they justify this outrage to the taxpayers who are keeping the company afloat?' and 'In the last six months, AIG has received substantial sums from the U.S. Treasury. I've asked Secretary Geithner to use that leverage and pursue every legal avenue to block these bonuses and make the American taxpayers whole.' Politicians on both sides of the Congressional aisle reacted with outrage to the planned bonuses. Senator Chuck Grassley (R-Iowa) said 'I would suggest the first thing that would make me feel a little bit better toward them if they'd follow the Japanese example and come before the American people and take that deep bow and say, I'm sorry, and then either do one of two things, resign or commit suicide. (Wikipedia, American International Group)

(11a) In the words of Matthew Karnitschnig et al, "Just last weekend, the government essentially pulled the plug on Lehman Brothers Holding Inc., allowing the big investment bank to go under instead of giving it financial support. This time, the government decided AIG truly was too big to fail.... It puts the government in control of a private insurer—a historic development, particularly considering that AIG isn't directly regulated by the federal government. The Fed took the highly unusual step using legal authority granted in the Federal Reserve Act, which allows it to lend to nonbanks under 'unusual and exigent' circumstances, something it invoked when Bear Sterns Cos was rescued in March. As part of the deal, Treasury Secretary Henry Paulson insisted that AIG's chief executive, Robert Willumstad, step aside. Mr. Paulson personally told Mr. Willumstad the news in a phone call on Tuesday according to a person familiar with the call. AIG's bailout caps a tumultuous 10 days that have remade the American financial system. In that time, the government has engineered rescues that insert it deep into the housing and insurance industries, while Wall Street has watched two of its last four big independent brokerage firms exit the scene. The U.S. on September 6 took over mortgage lending giants Fannie Mae and Freddie Mac as they teetered near collapse. This Sunday, the U.S. refused to bail out Wall Street pillar Lehman Brothers, which filed for bankruptcy-court protection and is now being sold off in pieces. That same day, another struggling Wall Street Titan, Merrill Lynch & Co., agreed to sell itself to Bank of America Corp. The AIG deal followed a day of high drama in Washington. The Treasury's Mr. Paulson and Federal Reserve Chairman Ben Bernanke convened in the early evening an expected meeting of top congressional leaders. Late in the trading day Tuesday, anticipation that the government might assist the insurer helped propel the Dow Jones Industrial Average to a 1.3% gain. In bailing out AIG, the Federal Reserve appeared to be motivated in part by worries that Wall Street financial crisis could begin to spill over into seemingly safe investments held by small investors, such as money-market funds that invest in AIG debt. Indeed, on Tuesday the $62 billion Primary Fund from the Reserve, a New York money-market firm, said it 'broke the buck'—that is, its net asset value fell below the $1-a—share level that funds like this must maintain. Breaking the buck is an extremely rare occurrence. The fund was pinched by investments in bonds issued by now collapsing Lehman Brothers. Money-market funds are supposed to be among the safest investments available. No fund in the $3.6 trillion money-market industry has lost money since 1994, when Orange County, Calif., went bankrupt. A number of money-market funds own securities issued by AIG. The firm is also a big insurer of some money-market instruments . . . . Staff from the Federal Reserve and Treasury worked on the plan through Monday night. President George W. Bush was briefed on the rescue Tuesday afternoon during a meeting of the President's Working Group on Financial Markets. That the Government would prop up AIG financially offers a stark indication of the breath of the insurer's role in the global economy. If it were to have trouble meeting its obligations, the potential domino effect could reach around the world. For one thing, banks and mutual funds are major holders of AIG's debt and could take a hit if the insurer were to default. In addition, AIG was a major seller of 'credit-default-swaps,' essentially insurance against default on assets tied to corporate debt and mortgage securities. Weakness at AIG could force financial institutions in the U.S., Europe and Asia that bought these swaps to take write-downs or losses. AIG's millions of insurance policyholders appear to be considerably less at risk. That's because of how the company is structured and regulated. Its insurance policies are issued by separate subsidiaries of AIG, highly regulated units that have assets available to pay claims. In the U.S. those assets can't be shifted out of the subsidiaries without regulatory approval, and insurance is also regulated strictly abroad." (Karnitschnig, 2008)

SOLYNDRA—(SCANDAL AND BANKRUPTCY)

(12) Wikipedia illustrates, "Solyndra was a manufacturer of cylindrical panels of Copper indium gallium selenite (CIGS) thin film solar cells based in Fremont, California. Although the company was once touted for its unusual technology, plummeting silicon prices led to the company being unable to compete with more conventional solar panels. On September 1, 2011, the company ceased all business activity, filed for Chapter 11 bankruptcy, and laid off all employees. The company is also being sued by employees who were abruptly laid off. Solyndra designed, manufactured and sold solar photovoltaic (PV) systems composed of panels and mounting hardware for large, low-slope commercial rooftops. The panels perform optimally when mounted horizontally and packed closely together, thereby, the company claimed, covering significantly more of the typically available roof area and producing more electricity per rooftop on an annual basis than a conventional panel installation. In 2006 Solyndra began deploying demonstration systems globally. The company stated the total count was 14 systems and that these systems were each instrumented with sensitive radiation, wind speed, temperature, and humidity measurement devices to aid in the development of energy yield forecasting software tools. The company's website claimed there were more than 1,000 Solyndra systems installed around the world, representing 100 megawatts of power. Solyndra was led by Brian Harrison, a veteran of Intel Corporation. He took the reins on July 27, 2010 when founder Chris Gronet was replaced as CEO. In 2009, the company posted $100 million in revenue. It was estimated that its production and sales growth could lead to a market cap between $1.76—2billion. 2010 revenues were approximately $140 million. Solyndra loan approval process began under the Bush administration. However, emails show that two weeks before Obama took office, the Energy Department panel considering the loan unanimously decided not to proceed. In March 2009, one White House budget analyst wrote an email stating that "This deal is NOT ready for primetime." However, Solyndra was the first company approved for a loan guarantee under the Obama administration. On March 20, 2009 the United States Department of Energy made a "conditional commitment" to a $535 million loan guarantee to support Solyndra's construction of a commercial-scale manufacturing plant for its proprietary solar photovoltaic panels. The White House scheduled a press event for September 4 and federal reviewers gave final on September 2. After

securing the loan guarantee, the Federal Financing Bank, a part of the Department of the Treasury, loaned Solyndra $527 million. The taxpayers are not expected to recover much of that money. Solyndra also received $25.1 million tax break from California's Alternative Energy and Advanced Transportation Financing Authority. The majority of Solyndra funding was provided under the Title XVII section 1705 of the Energy Policy Act of 2005 (as amended by the American Recovery and Reinvestment Act.) Title 1705 has provided $36 billion in loan guarantees for renewable energy projects. As of May 16, 2012 loan defaults had accounted for losses equivalent to roughly 2% of the loans provided under section 1705. In 2012 President Obama's chief strategist, David Axelrod responded to questions about the Department of Energy loan to Solyndra. He said that the Obama administration 'won't back off' over its clean energy policy. "It's good for the planet, it's good for the economy, and will create jobs . . . high end manufacturing jobs. This is going to continue being a thrust for us. He added that President Obama's first 2012 campaign ad, defending his clean energy policy, was a response to an ad sponsored by a Super PAC mentioning Solyndra. Republican presidential candidate Mitt Romney visited the empty Solyndra factory in mid-2012 as his campaign shifted from the primaries toward the convention and the general election. He criticized the bankruptcy and President Obama's previous support. Soon after Romney's visit to Solyndra another solar energy company, Konarka, declared bankruptcy. As Solyndra, Konarka had received federal financial support. But Konarka also had received 2002 financial support from the Massachusetts Governor Romney's administration. As such Konarka became something of a counterpoint to Solyndra in the political exchange with the Democratic President. [No need to wonder anymore, why the Republicans, especially Mitt Romney don't dare to make Solyndra an issue in an election year.] Shutdown and Investigation.—On August 31, 2011 Solyndra announced it was filing for Chapter 11 bankruptcy protection, laying off 1100 employees, and shutting down all operations and manufacturing, while providing no severance for the fired employees, or even providing back due vacation day credit. Solyndra's quarterly employee meetings told employees that the company was losing money, and that the production costs, while declining, were still higher than the also declining market prices for solar panels. The decision to lay off employees and cease operations came about as a result of a board meeting on August 30, in which terms for the injection of additional capital could not be agreed upon. This left Solyndra with virtually no cash. On September

8, 2011, Solyndra was raided by the FBI investigating the company. In September 2011, federal agents visited the homes of Brian Harrison, the company's CEO, and Chris Gronet, the company's founder, to examine computer files and documents. Also in September 2011, the U.S. Treasury Department launched an investigation. On September 29, 2011, a Treasury Department official confirmed that the criminal probe of Solyndra is focused on whether the company and its officer misrepresented the firm's finances to the government in seeking the loan or engaged in accounting fraud. On October 7, 2011, newly revealed emails showed that the Obama administration had concerns about the legality of the Energy Department's loan restructuring plan and warned OMB director Jeffrey D. Zients that the plan should be cleared with the Justice Department first, which the Energy Department had not done. The emails also revealed that as early as August 2009, an aide to then White House Chief of Staff Rahm Emanuel had asked an Energy Department official if he could discuss any concerns among the investment community about Solyndra but that the official dismissed the idea that Solyndra had financial problems. On Thursday, 13 October 2011, bankruptcy court approved the hiring of the chief restructuring officer Todd Neilson. (Wikipedia, Solyndra, 2012)

THE SOLAR SECTOR—GONE BELLYUP

(13) Yuliya Chernova asserts, "Long viewed as a remedy for the world's dependence on fossil fuels, the solar industry is dimming as makers of panels used to harness the sun continue to fall by the wayside. Bankruptcies, plummeting stock prices and crushing debt loads are calling into question the viability of an industry that since the 1970's has been counted on to advance the U.S.—and the world—into a new energy age. Global demand for solar power is still growing—about 8% more solar panels will be installed this year compared to 2010, according to Jefferies Group analysis—but it is expected to flat line next year. At the heart of the industry woes are swiftly falling prices for solar panels and their components—polysilicon, wafers, cells and the modules themselves. The reason is simple: There are simply too many manufacturers trying to sell their wares. Over the past several months, at least seven solar panel manufacturers have filed for bankruptcy or insolvency, including two German companies in the past week—Solar Millennium AG and Solon SE—and, most notably, Solyndra LLC, the Fremont, Calif. Company embroiled in a criminal investigation into

whether the company defrauded the U.S. Government. [Clearly, this article proves that there was no conspiracy theory between Solyndra and President Obama's Administration; and that the Solar Energy Companies were failing worldwide. The opposition Republican Party was just out to discredit and embarrass the Democrats. If Solyndra accepted the $535 million federally guaranteed loan knowing beforehand that the company was going belly-up and that their intention was to declare bankruptcy one day after receiving that loan; then their officers will most likely be investigated and prosecuted. This has been a very hot political issue that has continued, and will continue into the 2012 national elections.] Of the ten largest publicly traded companies by market capitalization whose focus is making solar components, six reported losses in the third quarter, and all but one of these ten produced weaker profits from a year earlier. Underscoring how debt is weighing down the industry, six of the ten also had debt on their balance sheets that exceeded their market capitalizations. Many more manufacturers are in a precarious financial situation, such as Energy Conversion Devices Inc., whose stock has nose-dived by 95% this year as the Auburn Hills, Michigan Company has suspended factory operations, deferred interest payments and restructured its staff. Energy Conversion couldn't be reached for comment. Overall, public market investors are punishing the solar sector, sending shares down nearly 57% this year as of Dec. 19, according to investment bank Stifel Nicholaus, compared with a decline of 3% for the S&P 500. Even First Solar Inc., the darling of the industry, is restructuring amid weaker results and project delays. In a Dec. 14 call with analyst that Jeff Osborne, an analyst with Stifel Nicholaus, said 'seemed like the funeral for the whole sector,' Mike Ahearn, First Solar chairman and interim CEO, said the industry will suffer pricing pressures indefinitely. This means the shakeout among manufacturers will likely continue for some time. 'The industry simply cannot support 300-plus cell and modular manufacturers,' said Zhengrong Shi, chief executive of Chinese solar-panel manufacturer Sun-Tech Power Holdings Co., during a late-November call with investors. Sun Tech is cutting its operating expenses by at least 20% next year as it hopes to stem this year's 70% stock-price slide. The glut of manufacturers stems from various sources over the last several years, including efforts by the U.S. government to encourage clean technology, venture capitalists pouring into the sector and institutional investors buying into IPO issues of solar companies amid an oil price boom and a heightened sense of climate change urgency. At the same time European governments offered rich subsidies for solar installation, driving demand in the market. 'People were doing what they can to make a profit, without thinking ahead,' said Pallavi Madakasira, an analyst with research firm Lux Research Inc. But the biggest factor was the decision by the Chinese government to direct its banks to lend freely to new manufacturers a few years ago. Since 2009, Chinese banks have offered at least $43 billion in credit facilities to Chinese renewable-energy companies, according to Bloomberg New Energy Finance. It isn't clear how much of that money has been drawn down, but the easy access to capital during the height of the global credit crunch allowed Chinese companies to build factories and start production, forcing competitors in Europe and the U.S. to do the same. The plentiful production of solar panels resulted in a cut-throat pricing competition. A year ago, customers—mostly distributors of panels and project developers—could by solar panels for $1.60 per watt, on average. Now the going price is between 90 cents to $1.05 per watt, according to investment bank Jefferies. Meanwhile, U.S. trade authorities are investigating domestic manufacturers' complaints over possible dumping of solar panels on the U.S. market by Chinese makers. Despite the buyers' market, customers aren't opening their wallets fast enough. In Europe, which buys more solar panels than any other region, banks clamped up on funding, and customers wound up with warehouses full of solar panels, causing them to defer additional orders. Many are also wary about committing to new solar contracts while prices keep falling. Germany, for years the world's largest market for solar, is seeing a 29% decline in demand this year over 2010, according to Jefferies. That is quite a contrast to 2010, when installations in Germany nearly doubled. Meanwhile, in the U.S. demand has actually risen because utilities have been buying solar power to fill state mandates, while large plant projects continue to attract investment from companies such as Google Inc., NRG Energy Inc., and MidAmerican Energy Co. That growth may not be sustainable, however, because the mandates for renewable energy are quickly being fulfilled. And if solar is getting cheaper, so too is competing natural-gas power." (Chernova, 2011)

MF GLOBAL—(JON CORZINE)

(14) "On Sunday, October 30, 2011 a unit of the New York based brokerage first reported to the Chicago Mercantile Exchange (CME) and the Commodities Futures Trading Commission (CFTC) a 'material shortfall' of hundreds of millions of dollars in segregated customer

funds. Customer accounts were frozen the same day and the parent company, MF Global Inc., filed the eight-largest U.S. Bankruptcy. MF Global would ultimately report the shortfall in customer accounts at $891,465,650 as of close of business Friday, October 28, 2011. According to the trustee overseeing liquidation and shortfall may be as large as $1.6 billion. MF Global mixed customer funds and used them for its own account for at least several days before the bankruptcy and transferred funds outside the country. The liquidation trustee ultimately reported that on October 26, 2011. Edith O'Brien, an assistant treasurer in Chicago who reported to the firm's treasurer in New York approved transfers totaling $615 million from segregated customer trust accounts at JPMorgan Chase, supposedly for an intra-day loan. The funds weren't returned by the end of the day, causing panic in Ms. O'Brien's operation. Ms. O'Brien continued to approve such 'loans' in the ensuing days. On the morning of October 28, two company officials noted a deficit in segregated customer accounts of about $300 million. Two members of Ms. O'Brien's staff improperly determined that a $540 million wire transfer into the segregated accounts the previous day had somehow gone unrecorded and double counted the transfer. The firm reported a surplus of more than $200 million to the commodities commission. The segregation report was revised to show a surplus without any backup documentation. The same day, the 28th, CEO Jon Corzine ordered Ms. O'Brien to transfer $175 million to JPMorgan to cover a firm overdraft. With no other source for cash, Ms. O'Brien approved a transfer of $200 million from a customer trust account at JPMorgan. The trustee's report concludes there was a substantial 'shortfall' in customer segregated funds every day from Oct.26th, when $615 million in loans from customer accounts were not repaid, until MF Global filed for bankruptcy on Oct. 31st. The CME reports that early on Monday, October 31st, 2011, officials of MF Global admitted transfer of $700 million from customer accounts to the broker-dealer and a loan of $175 million in customer funds to MF Global's U.K. subsidiary to cover or mask liquidity shortfalls at the company. The brokerage used a large number of complex and controversial repurchase agreements or 'repos' for funding and for leveraging profit, many off their balance sheet. Some of these complex repos have been described as a wrong-way $6.3 billion trade MF Global made on its own behalf on bonds of some of Europe's most indebted nations. Failure of the repo positions helped cause the liquidity crisis at the firm. The sudden disappearance of so much liquidity may indicate a scandal and crisis related to the widespread practice among U.S. and U.K. brokers of rehypothecation of customer collateral. Rehypothecation is not allowed in Canada and Canadian customers of MF Global were able to recover all their funds within ten days.... On Monday October 31st, 2011, MF Global filed for Chapter 11 bankruptcy. KPMG is now conducting the 'Special Administration' for MF Global U.K. The Wall Street Journal reported that MF Global would seek Chapter 11 bankruptcy protection after investing $6 billion in sovereign bonds issued by European countries. According to the CME Group Inc., MF Global broke rules on keeping customer money separate from its own trading accounts. On August 31st 2011 MF Global had $7.3 billion in customer assets, according to Commodities Futures Trading Commission data. The MF Global bankruptcy was the largest Wall Street firm to collapse since the Lehman Brothers incident in September 2008." (Wikipedia, MF Global)

(14a) Aaron Lucchetti of WSJ blogs asserts, "MF Global' CEO, Jon Corzine, spent about nine months building up a huge bet on European bonds that helped torpedo the company. It took about two weeks for the position to be liquidated. Last week, LCH Clearnet, a London based clearing house that helped arranged the trades, finished liquidating the rest of MF Global $6.3 billion in European sovereign bond exposure, according to Richard Heis, one of the joint special administrators at KPMG LLP that is working on winding down MF Global's U.K. business. At the time of the Oct. 31 bankruptcy, MF Global had sold about $1.5 billion in the portfolio. That left close to $5 billion in remaining bets on European bonds of Portugal, Italy, Ireland, Belgium and Spain. Disclosure about the position earlier in October sparked fear among customers, lenders and investors that led to a run on the bank the last week of the month. KPMG's Mr. Heis said the position was sold at a loss, but that it would have been worse had the position not been liquidated when Italian bond yields surged versus comparable bonds last Wednesday. Mr. Heis also said he is hopeful that at least one or two parts of the company's U.K. and European business can be sold, potentially helping creditors and customers who have lost money in the firm's collapse". (LCH Clearnet Finishes Unloading Corzine's European Bet, 2011)

(14b) Devlin Barrett contends that, "Federal prosecutors in Chicago and New York have issued subpoenas in the probe of the collapse of MF Global Holdings Ltd., people familiar with the case said, a sign of an intensifying Justice Department criminal investigation as authorities try to track down about $600 million in client funds. Chicago U.S. Attorney Patrick Fitzgerald and New York U.S. Attorney Preet Bharara, regarded as two of most aggressive and high-profile federal prosecutors in the country, are using subpoenas to gather company records, the people familiar with the matter said. The Justice Department and the FBI are conducting a criminal investigation of MF Global's collapse. Other federal regulators are also investigating. A lawyer for MF Global, Kenneth S. Ziman of Skadden, Arps, Slate, Meagher, & Flom LLP, said at a hearing Wednesday in U.S. Bankruptcy Court in Manhattan that the company was 'besieged' by demands from regulators for documents and evidence. MF Global filed for Chapter 11 bankruptcy protection on Oct. 31 after a rapid implosion, leaving questions about the whereabouts of the roughly $600 million apparently missing from customer accounts. Mr. Fitzgerald's office moved first, issuing subpoenas almost immediately after the bankruptcy filing, according to the people familiar with the case. The initial subpoenas to MF Global were issued in part out of a desire to ensure no business records were destroyed or lost in the company's chaotic collapse they said. No one has been charged with any wrongdoing. Meanwhile, the senior commodities regulator overseeing the investigation into the missing funds said she is more focused on returning the money to customers than figuring out how it disappeared. 'Trying to figure out who started the fire is not really my goal right now,' Jill Sommers, a member of the Commodity Futures Trading Commission, said in an interview. 'I need to get the people out of the building.' The CFTC is the primary regulator for MF Global's large futures-trading operation, though the firm also is overseen by the Securities and Exchange Commission and Financial Industry Regulatory Authority. Ms. Sommers said the CFTC is supporting the trustee overseeing MF Global's liquidation on anything he can do outside the regular bankruptcy claims process to get customer funds returned. Court-appointed trustee James Giddens sought court approval to release about $520 million in customer cash still held at the failed firm, according to a court filing late Tuesday. If approved, the move would ease the strain on former MF Global clients whose money has been locked up for weeks in the New York firm's bankruptcy". (U.S. Levels Subpoenas In Probe of MF Global, 11/17/2011)

(14c) Scott Patterson et al argue that, "Jon S. Corzine defended his tenure as chief executive of MF Global Holdings Ltd. Before a House Committee, but couldn't explain an estimated $1.2 million in missing customer money. Visibly tense in the politically charged hearing, Mr. Corzine 64 years old, on Tuesday told the House Agriculture Committee that he has been 'devastated by the enormous impact on many peoples' lives' caused by MF Global's collapse. 'I simply do not know where the money is,' he said in response to questions from the panel, noting that 'there were an extraordinary number of transactions during MF Global's last few days' and that he didn't know everything that was going on. Pressed for an answer as to what could have happened, he said that it was possible, though unlikely, that underlings might have misunderstood an order and mistakenly dipped into customer funds. [Imagine that this is a former Senator, a former Governor of the State of New Jersey, and an Executive of a Major Trading Company giving this lame excuse and sounding less like that of an intellectual. Anyone, who hold an executive position in a major trading company, along with officers of the company must know that one of the golden rules established: is that there is to be no co-mingling of customer funds with that of the corporations'. Given his accomplishments, Mr. Corzine is no fool. Sooner or later, the truth about the missing funds will be discovered. Where was the Back-Office? Who was supervising the underlings? Were they always unsupervised and needed no authorization to dip into customers' accounts? Were the underlings allowed to independently churn customers' accounts? There seemed to be an astounding absence of accountability.] Mr. Corzine said he still expects that the money eventually will be found and recovered. Mr. Corzine resigned as MF Global chairman and chief executive days after the firm's Oct. 31 bankruptcy filing. Speaking in a deep, raspy voice, the former New Jersey Senator and Governor and Goldman Sachs Group Inc., chairman appeared as befuddled by what had happened to his firm as the regulators who have been attempting to resolve the matter for more than a month. It was his first public appearance since the firm's collapse. Frequently stroking his trademark beard and fumbling with his prepared testimony, Mr. Corzine argued that MF Global was felled not by its $6.3 billion bet on European debt, but rather by a sudden lack of confidence in its balance sheet by the broader market in October. As counterparts and clients grew nervous about MF Global's financial strength, they pulled money out of the firm. That triggered a fatal crisis of liquidity. Referencing an October 17 Wall Street Journal article reporting that regulators had been concerned about MF Global's balance sheet over the summer, Mr. Corzine said 'the marketplace lost confidence in the firm.' Mr. Corzine said he first learned of the missing money at about 10 p.m. Sunday, Oct. 30, as the firm was attempting to close a deal to sell assets to

Interactive Brokers Group Inc. He said that he was 'stunned' when he learned of the shortfall and that his first response was to tell his staff 'go back and check your work.' Investors believe that MF Global, in the week before it filed for bankruptcy protection, moved funds from the customer accounts to its broker-dealer operations, which handled the European-bond bet, according to people familiar with the matter. Futures Firms such as MF Global are prohibited from using customer cash in their own accounts, according to the Commodity Exchange Act. The Federal Bureau of Investigation is currently investigating the firm's collapse. When Mr. Corzine was asked Thursday about whether customer money was moved, he answered the question indirectly, saying 'I never intended to break any rules.' A few seconds later, he gave a slightly more specific response, saying that he didn't intend to direct customer money out of segregated accounts." (Patterson, 12/09/2011)

(14d) Aaron Lucchetti et al concludes that, "Investigators on the hunt for an estimated $1.2 billion in customer money missing since MF Global Holdings Ltd. Collapsed are zeroing in on the securities firm's back-office operations in Chicago, people familiar with the situation said. One back-office employee have told people she disputes congressional testimony by Jon S. Corzine, MF Global's former chairman and chief executive, that she provided assurance that a $200 million transfer was proper, according to people familiar with the matter. Civil and Criminal regulators have 'talked to a lot of people' in the Chicago office which handled day-to-day movement of money for MF Global, including a $6 billion customer-segregated account that was tapped shortly before the company filed for bankruptcy-court protection Oct. 31, according to a person close to the investigation. Some of the roughly 700 employees have been 'approached by everyone and their mother' since regulators swept into the building two months ago, this person said. In contrast, federal prosecutors haven't interviewed Mr. Corzine, operations Chief Bradley I. Abelow or Chief Financial Officer Henri J. Steenkamp, top executives who worked at the securities firm's headquarters in New York, according to people familiar with the matter. [Wonder Why? Was it because of Mr. Corzine's political clout and his influence with the people he knew in Washington?] Messrs. Corzine, Abelow, and Steenkamp haven't been accused of wrongdoing. It isn't clear how much progress the Justice Department, two U.S. Attorneys Offices, Commodities Futures Trading Commission, Securities and Exchange Commission and other regulators have made as a result of the scrutiny in Chicago, ranging from accountants to controllers to treasury officials.

Nestled between the Chicago Board of Trade and the elevated train in the city's financial district, the back-office was responsible for making sure that customer futures accounts were handled properly. Another floor housed MF Global salesmen. People close to the probe said investigators are pushing hard to determine which Chicago back-office employees knew about movement of money in the days before MF Global tumbled into bankruptcy protection, who ordered certain money transfers and if anyone knew that the transfers would lead to a shortfall in the customer-segregated accounts. As company officials tried in late October to overcome a customer exodus and demands for more collateral from counterparties, numerous MF Global employees in Chicago stayed at work around the clock, a person familiar with the situation said. The back-office employee who has disputed Mr. Corzine's testimony is Assistant Treasurer Edith O'Brien. She has told people that she disagrees with Mr. Corzine's suggestion at a House Subcommittee Hearing in December that she provided assurance that a $200 million transfer to J.P. Morgan Chase & Co., three days before the bankruptcy-protection filing was proper, according to people familiar with the situation. She has declined to be interviewed by a House subcommittee and the Justice Department and is seeking immunity from prosecution in exchange for cooperation, said people familiar with the matter. Ms. O'Brien, who couldn't be reached for comment, still works for a trustee now unwinding the company. Mr. Corzine testified that he got 'assurance from our back-office people in Chicago,' including Ms. O'Brien, that the transfer complied with all the relevant rules. [What a bunch of malarkey coming from company officials that should know Stock Exchange Rules and Regulations.] The transfer was needed to cover an overdraft in an MF Global account at J.P. Morgan. The former Goldman Sachs Group Inc. Chairman, U.S. senator and New Jersey governor said the 'back-office in Chicago explicitly confirmed to me that the funds were properly transferred.' At the same hearing Mr. Corzine said Ms. O'Brien was the person he spoke to about the issue. Mr. Corzine, who declined to comment through a spokesman, has said he never directed anyone at MF Global to misuse customer funds. Ms. O'Brien hasn't been accused of wrongdoing. It isn't clear what Ms. O'Brien's role in the transfer was or why she has disputed Mr. Corzine's testimony. A letter sent from J.P. Morgan to MF Global the next day was addressed to her and began with 'Dear Edith,' according to a copy reviewed by The Wall Street Journal. The letter from J.P. Morgan Managing Director Donna Dellosso, asked MF Global to 'acknowledge and confirm that the transfer and withdrawal out of such

Customer Segregated Account for the purpose of covering overdraft amounts in accounts with J.P. Morgan represented your actual interest in such funds' and were 'made in accordance with the provisions' of U.S. commodities laws and rules. At the bottom are two blanks where MF Global was supposed to indicate it 'acknowledged and agreed' that the $200 million transfer was proper, according to the copy of the letter reviewed by the Journal. No one ever signed the letter, a person with the matter said. In addition to Ms. O'Brien, investigators have expressed interest in talking to Christy Vavra, who ran MF Global's treasury operations and helped handle the movement of customer money, according to a person familiar with the situation. Another person of interest to investigators is Christine Serwinski, who worked with Ms. O'Brien in MF Global's Chicago office. Ms. Serwinski was the company's North American finance chief. Mr. Corzine told lawmakers last month that Ms. Serwinski was 'at the very top' of employees who oversaw customer funds, though she was on vacation for part of the week leading up to MF Global's bankruptcy filing. Ms. Vavra and Ms. Serwinski haven't been accused of wrongdoing. At the time of MF Global's collapse, Ms. Serwinski had told friends that she planned to leave the securities firm in early 2012, according to people familiar with the matter. Ms. Serwinski and Ms. Vavra couldn't be reached for comment." (Lucchetti A. S., 01/17/2012)

RAJ RAJARATNAM, HEDGE FUND BILLIONAIRE

(15) Wikipedia claims, "Raj Rajaratnam, born June 15, 1957 is a Sri Lankan-American and former hedge fund manager and founder of the Galleon Group, a New York based hedge fund Management firm. On October 16, 2009 he was arrested by the FBI on allegations of insider trading, which also caused the Galleon Group to close. He stood trial in U.S. v Rajaratnam (09 Cr. 01184) in the United States District Court for the Southern District of New York, and on May 11, 2011 was found guilty on all 14 counts of conspiracy and securities fraud. (Wikipedia, Raj Rajaratnam, 2012)

(15a) Washington Post Reporter David S. Hilzenrath summarizes, "Raj Rajaratnam, the hedge fund billionaire at the center of one of the largest insider trading cases in history, was sentenced Thursday to 11 years in prison. It was the longest prison term ever for insider trading, according to the Justice Department, and was the culmination of a years-long federal probe of cheating in the stock market. But it was also substantially less than what the prosecution had sought against the man it called 'a billion-dollar force of deception and corruption on Wall Street.' The 54-year-old Rajaratnam, who headed Galleon Management, <u>was convicted in May</u> on 14 counts of conspiracy and securities fraud for illegally using inside information to trade in stocks such as <u>Goldman Sachs, Google, Hilton and Intel.</u> The trading generated profits or avoided losses of $72 million, the government estimated. The case pulled back the curtain on illicit trafficking in corporate secrets that involved people at the highest echelons of the financial world and gave hedge funds a competitive edge. The 11 year sentence reflects a trend toward tougher treatment of insider-trading convicts, said former federal prosecutor Robert W. Ray. Less than a decade ago, it would have been unusual for a defendant in a major insider trading case to get more than two years, Ray said. Rajaratnam's crimes 'reflect a virus in our business culture that needs to be eradicated,' U.S. District Judge Richard J. Holwell said at the sentencing in New York. 'It is a sad conclusion to what once seemed to be a glittering story,' Manhattan U.S. Attorney Preet Bharara said in a news release. Bharara said he hoped the case served as a wakeup call. 'Privileged professionals do not get a free pass to pursue profit through corrupt means,' he said. Rajaratnam was ordered to forfeit $53.4 million and pay a fine of $10 million. Out on $100 million bail, he is scheduled to report for prison on Nov. 28. The Justice Department opposed allowing Rajaratnam to stay out of prison while he appeals, saying he might flee to his native Sri Lanka or some other country. He 'would have access to tens of millions of dollars by the mere touch of a keystroke,' the government said in a court filing. Rajaratnam will appeal his conviction, Kathryn Holmes Johnson, a spokesman for his legal team, said by e-mail. The Associated Press reported from New York that defense lawyers asked that Rajaratnam be allowed to go the medical facility at the Butner Federal Correctional Complex in North Carolina, where Bernard Madoff is serving his 150-year sentence for running a Ponzi scheme that cheated thousands of people out of billions of dollars. Though Rajaratnam did not testify at his trial, the prosecution made extensive use of wiretaps of his conversations with associates. According to the government, Rajaratnam gathered inside information about pending corporate deals and earnings announcements form an array of tipsters, including a Goldman Sachs board member, a senior partner at the consulting firm McKinsey & Co. and an insider at the Moody's credit rating agency. To pay for inside information, Rajaratnam wired money to offshore accounts in phony names, the government said.

He lied under oath when called in for questioning by the Securities and Exchange Commission, told others to use prepaid cellphones and created false e-mails as cover stories to disguise the basis for his trades, the government said. The Justice Department had urged the court to sentence Rajaratnam to at least 19 years and seven months and as much as 24 years and five months. Such a term was warranted to 'provide just and fair punishment for perhaps the worst insider trading offender' caught to date 'and deter others,' the Justice Department wrote. Defense lawyers had countered that the sentence the government sought 'would ensure Mr. Rajaratnam's death in prison—a fate ordinarily reserved only for offenders who have caused the most grave, irreversible, and demonstrable harm to others'. Rajaratnam 'suffers from a constellation of serious and degenerative illness which require intensive ongoing medical attention and which under the best of circumstances will almost certainly shorten his life considerably,' they said in a court filing. In determining the sentence, Holwell cited Rajaratnam's need for a kidney transplant and his advanced diabetes, the AP reported. The judge also credited Rajaratnam's charity work, which he called 'the defendant's responsiveness to and care for the less privileged.' [Seriously, can anyone in good conscience honestly state that Rajaratnam had a good heart or was a kind and generous gentleman? Was he really a hedge-fund billionaire—turned modern day Robin Hood that made billions of dollars in illicit gains in front-running just to give to the poor? What a cop-out and an excuse to be as lenient as possible in handing down a pity-sentence. Perhaps Rajaratnam was being generous with his ill-gotten gains, so that he could be viewed as a kind-hearted and an honest individual. However, his shady dealings soon caught up with him.] Asked if he wish to speak, Rajaratnam said only, 'No, thank you, your honor,' according to AP. The insider trading case was the most prominent of its kind since Ivan Boesky was convicted a generation ago. Rajaratnam will join a list of high-profile white-collar financial figures sent to prison, including former Enron executive Jeffrey Skilling, former WorldCom executive Bernard Ebbers and Ponzi scheme mastermind Madoff. The federal system offers no possibility of parole and only limited credit for good behavior, so it is likely that Rajaratnam will be locked up for at least nine years, said Douglas A. Berman, a law professor at Ohio State University who specializes in criminal sentencing. Berman said he was surprised that Rajaratnam's sentence 'was as low as it was.' As a deterrent, 'there's reasons to worry this isn't going to move the needle much,' Berman said. Sentences for insider-trading tend to be significantly lighter than the punishments meted out in major accounting frauds, said Michael Perino, a professor at the St. John's University School of Law. That might be because the economic impact of insider trading is more diffused and impersonal than the fallout from accounting frauds such as Enron's, in which employees lost jobs and particular investors lost huge sums of money, Perino said. WorldCom's Ebbers was sentenced to 25 years. Enron's Skilling was originally sentenced to 24 years but is waiting resentencing based on an appeal." (Hilzenrath, 2011)

RAJAT GUPTA—SECURITIES FRAUD

(16) Wikipedia contends this, "Rajat Kumar Gupta, Bengali, born 2 December 1948, is an Indian-American businessman who was the managing director (chief executive) of management consultancy McKinsey & Company from 1944 to 2003 and a business leader in India and the United States. He was arrested in late 2011 by the FBI on insider trading charges stemming from the Raj Rajaratnam Galleon Group case and is scheduled for criminal trial in May 2012. In his capacity at McKinsey, Gupta was recognized as the first Indian-born CEO of a global corporation. After retiring from active practice, while maintaining an affiliation at McKinsey, Gupta served as corporate chairman, board director or strategic advisor to a variety of large and notable organizations (full list): corporations including Goldman Sachs, Proctor and Gamble, and American Airlines, and non-profits including The Gates Foundation, The Global Fund, and the International Chamber of Commerce. Rajat Gupta is additionally the co-founder of four different organizations: the Indian School of Business with Anil Kumar, the America India Foundation with Victor Menezes and Lata Krishnan, New Silk Route with Parag Saxena and Menezes again, and Scandent with Ramesh Vangal. On October 26, 2011, Gupta was arrested by the Federal Bureau of Investigation on charges of securities fraud and conspiracy as part of an ongoing and wide-ranging insider trading case in which Gupta's close associates Raj Rajaratnam and Anil Kumar were convicted and pled guilty, respectively. The Securities and Exchange Commission (SEC) sued Gupta the same day. Gupta entered a plea of not guilty and was released on $10 million bail. Previously, from March to August 2011, the SEC had filed administrative suit against Gupta, been countersued by Gupta, and then dropped those charges. During that period, Gupta's conversations on tape with Rajaratnam, particularly those made while Gupta was a board member of Goldman Sachs, were played during

Rajaratnam's trial and attracted widespread attention and notoriety. In the lead up and wake of the original SEC charges, Gupta resigned the majority of his corporate and philanthropic positions. Rajat Gupta was born in Kolkata, India to Pran Kumari Gupta and Ashwini Kumar Gupta. His father was a journalist for Amanda Publishers. His father was a prominent freedom fighter and had been jailed by the British for his efforts. His mother taught at a Montessori school. Gupta had three siblings. When Gupta was five the family moved to New Delhi, where his father went to start the newspaper Hindustan Standard. Gupta's father died when Gupta was sixteen; Gupta's mother died two years later. Now an Orphan, Gupta and his siblings 'decided to live by ourselves. It was pretty unusual in those days.' He was a student at Modern School in New Delhi. After high school, Gupta ranked 15th in the nation in the entrance exam for the Indian Institutes of Technology. He received a Bachelor of Technology degree in Mechanical Engineering from the Indian Institute of Technology, Delhi in 1971. Declining a job from the prestigious domestic firm ITC Limited, he received an MBA from Harvard Business School in 1973, where he was named a Baker Scholar. Gupta remarked that the first time he saw an airplane was when he flew to ITC to inform them he would be attending HBS . . . . On March 1, 2011, the SEC levied administrative civil insider trading charges against Gupta. He was accused of passing material non-public information to Galleon Group's Raj Rajaratnam, who in U.S. v Rajaratnam was found guilty on all 14 counts of insider trading and securities fraud and sentenced to 11 years in prison. In the wake of the SEC accusations, Gupta resigned form or did not stand for reelection to the boards of Goldman Sachs, Proctor and Gamble, AMR and its subsidiary, American Airlines Inc., Harman International, and Genpact Ltd, among others. He also countersued the SEC and in August 2011 the charges and the countersuit were dropped by mutual agreement. [There were adequate taped telephone conversations, between Gupta and Rajaratnam to incriminate and bring Gupta to trial; so why did the SEC blink by mutually agreeing to drop the suit? Did Gupta have other influential forces backing him and pushing the SEC's back to the wall?] In September 2011 the Wall Street Journal indicated that criminal charges were imminent. In October 2011 the United States Attorney's Office formerly filed charges. Gupta surrendered to the FBI on October 26, 2011 and was released on $10 million bail. Gupta joined McKinsey & Company in 1973 as one of the earliest Indian-Americans at the consultancy. He was originally rejected because of inadequate work experience; a decision that was overturned after his Harvard Business School professor Walter J. Salmon called Ron Daniel, and then head of the New York office and later also the managing director of McKinsey, on Gupta's behalf. Gupta began his career in New York before moving to Scandinavia to become the head of McKinsey offices there in 1981. He did well in what was then considered a 'backwater' area; this is where he first made his mark. Elected senior partner in 1984, he became head of the Chicago office in 1990. In 1994 he was elected the firm's first managing director (chief executive) born outside of the U.S., and reelected twice in 1997 and 2000. In this capacity, he was considered the first Indian-born CEO of a multinational organization. After completing three full terms (the minimum allowed, by a rule he had himself initiated) and nearly a decade as head of the firm, Gupta became senior partner again in 2003 and retired from McKinsey as senior partner emeritus in 2007. Gupta is widely regarded as one of the first Indians to successfully break through the glass ceiling, as the first Indian-born CEO of a multinational corporation. Over a 34-year career at McKinsey, Gupta directed a number of projects aimed at helping companies develop new product/market strategies and reorganize for improved effectiveness and operations capabilities. He has a broad range of consulting experience with a variety of industries, including telecommunications, energy, and consumer goods . . . . Insider trading charges—On April 15, 2010, the Wall Street Journal reported that federal prosecutors in the United States were investigating Gupta's involvement in providing insider information to Galleon hedge-fund founder Raj Rajaratnam during the financial crisis, in particular the $5 billion Berkshire Hathaway investment in Goldman Sachs at the height of the financial crisis in September, 2008. Coverage of the event noted that Anil Kumar, [Kumar is another unsavory character who you will read of in the next excerpt. There ought to be serious scrutiny and better regulations of America's banks that caused the financial crisis that the nation experienced. However, having new regulations can only be effective if there are ample resources to deal with the infractions. The Treasury Department should stop favoring banks in preference to homeowners and investors, as was done with TARP.]—who like Gupta, had graduated from IIT, was a longtime highly-regarded senior partner at McKinsey, and had also co-founded the ISB—had already pleaded guilty to charges in the same case. Gupta, Kumar, and Rajaratnam were all close friends and business partners. When Goldman Sachs CEO Lloyd Blankfein asked Gupta about his insider trading rumors breaking in the press, Gupta replied,

'I wouldn't have had anything to do with that.' On March 19, 2010, it was announced that Gupta had decided not to stand for reelection to the Goldman Sachs board of directors. At the time this was seen as a reaction to the insider trading implications; however, wiretaps released over a year later in U.S. v Rajaratnam of Anil Kumar speaking to Rajaratnam reveal an anticipated conflict-of-interest with a senior advisory role at Kohlberg Kravis Roberts. Gupta has since stepped down as senior advisor to KKR. SEC v Gupta administrative suit—On March 1, 2011, the SEC filed an administrative civil complaint against Gupta for insider trading. It is alleged that he illegally tipped Rajaratnam with insider information about Goldman Sachs and Proctor and Gamble while having served on the boards of both companies. Rajaratnam, it is alleged, 'used the information from Gupta to illegally profit in hedge-fund trades . . . . The information on Goldman made Rajaratnam's funds $17 million richer . . . . The Proctor & Gamble data created illegal profits of more than $570,000 for Galleon funds managed by others,' the SEC said. After a Goldman Sachs board call . . . Mr. Gupta is said to have hung up the phone and called Mr. Rajaratnam 23 seconds later. The next morning, the SEC says, Galleon funds sold their Goldman holdings, avoiding losses of more than $3 million,' The New York Times continued. Gupta 'vigorously denied the SEC accusations.' He is being represented by respected white-collar criminal attorney Gary Naftalis of Kramer Levine Naftalis and Frankel LLP in connection with the charges. Mr. Naftalis 'strongly denied that Gupta had done anything wrong' in 2010 when Gupta's name was first mentioned relative to the case and said in March 2011 that the SEC charges were 'totally baseless.' Naftalis went on to say 'that Gupta is not accused of receiving anything in exchange for information provided and that Gupta lost his entire investment in Galleon by fall 2008.' The lost investment was specified to be 'USD 10 million . . . in Galleon Buccaneers Voyager Fund.' Gupta's counter suit claims he is the first person ever charged by SEC in this type of proceeding who is not a broker-dealer or investment management employee. Another important aspect of insider training is gain—Gupta's lawyer Naftalis said on March 1, that 'Gupta is not accused of receiving anything in exchange for information.' Yet a week later in U.S. v Rajaratnam it emerged that Mr. Rajaratnam . . . might pay Mr. Gupta with a large stake in the fund, and that Mr. Rajaratnam loaned Mr. Gupta money so he could increase his investment in a Galleon fund.' It also emerged that Mr. Gupta was in talks to become chairman of Galleon International, and therefore also stood to profit.

[That's real greed on the part of Mr. Gupta; after all he had practically everything. Why be tempted to go for chairman of Galleon fund? Here is a man with a stellar career, a Harvard Business Graduate, and a millionaire times over. Why risk throwing so much away to possibly be banned from the industry, spend time in prison, and destroy his reputation?] Wiretaps in U.S. v Rajaratnam were later played of Gupta asking Rajaratnam, 'I want . . . us to keep having the dialog as to . . . how I can be helpful in Galleon International and Galleon Group.' After Rajaratnam's conviction and the revelations about Gupta in the Rajaratnam trial, the difficulty of SEC's proving even the civil charges against Gupta was still deemed considerable by observers. Among other aspects, the May 2011, Bloomberg reported that, remarkably none of Gupta's alleged criminal tips to Rajaratnam appear to have been captured on the FBI's wiretaps.' But the report also noted a March 2010 e-mail from Gupta to Ajit Rangnekar, dean of the Indian School of Business, with denials, assertions and, in the reporter's opinion, 'obvious inaccuracies,' leaving many questions on how the cases and story would yet unfold." (Wikipedia, Rajat Gupta, 2012)

ANIL KUMAR—INSIDER TRADING

(17) Wikipedia points out that, "Anil Kumar (born 1958) was a longtime top senior partner and director at management consultancy McKinsey & Company, the co-founder of the Indian School of Business with Rajat Gupta, and the creator of two different types of outsourcing. He graduated from the Doon School and the Indian Institute of Technology Bombay in India, Imperial College London in the UK, and the Wharton School in the US. In 2010 he pleaded guilty to insider trading in a dramatic 'descent from the pinnacle of the business world. Kumar was 'one of McKinsey's most senior employees and brightest stars,' where he pioneered the concepts of Knowledge Process Outsourcing and Business Process Outsourcing. He was a protégé of longtime former managing director (chief executive) Rajat Gupta, though following Gupta's retirement never ran in the elections for chief executive himself. Anticipating the rise of India and Silicon Valley, he co-founded (and later directed) McKinsey offices in Silicon Valley in the 1980s and in India in the 1990s. During the dot-com bubble he headed McKinsey's technology and Internet Consulting operations, where he and Gupta created a program to allow the firm to accept stock in lieu of consulting fees. At McKinsey Kumar was also chairman of the Knowledge Center and Chairman of the Asia Center. He was director

and corporate officer of the firm. He lived and worked from multiple offices in New Delhi, New York, and Silicon Valley, travelling over thirty thousand miles a month. Kumar co-founded the Indian School of Business in 1997, today ranked among the top 15 business schools in the world by The Financial Times. He is a member of the Council on Foreign Relations and the Young Presidents' Organization, a founding charter member of TiE, and was the US chairman of India's largest business lobby, the Confederation of Indian Industry. Criticism of Kumar centered on his close relationship with Gupta and a perception of arrogance. According to *The Financial Times*, 'the two operated as a forceful double-act to secure business for McKinsey, <u>win access in Washington and build a brotherhood of donors</u> [Are we talking lobbyist here?] Around the Hyderabad-based ISB and a handful of social initiatives. Also, 'as much as Mr. Kumar was admired for his business ability and sharpness, he also drew fire for what was seen as his arrogance.' [Raj Rajaratnam, Rajat Gupta, and Anil Kumar were no ordinary men. They were all very educated, influential and respected men, millionaires—who, the more they acquired, the greedier they got as partners in crime.] The Galleon Case—Kumar remained hidden from the media and outside McKinsey until an October 2009 arrest in conjunction with an ongoing and wide-ranging US governmental investigation into insider trading. Former mentor Rajat Gupta was later arrested by the FBI in a related case, prompting inquiries into McKinsey's senior leadership and business model. As of December 2009, Kumar was no longer at the consultancy. In January 2010 he pleaded guilty to insider trading charges and was the government's star witness in March 2011 in US v Rajaratnam against his billionaire friend and Galleon Group founder Raj Rajaratnam. In the sprawling case his involvement was unusual; according to a Reuters blog. 'He's the only information who could be considered even more successful than Raj was, at least professionally if not in terms of raw cash. Raj had money, more money than he really knew what to do with, but Kumar had much more societal acceptance and prestige. He settled with the SEC in May 2010 for $2.8 million, the amount after gains he received form Rajaratnam through a Swiss bank account in a domestic worker's name. Gupta, Rajaratnam, and Kumar were all close friends and had founded the $1.3 billion private equity firm New Silk Route together, though Rajaratnam and Kumar withdrew before the firm began operation. Kumar was represented by respected attorney Robert Morvillo, who had previously led billionaire Martha Stewart's defense in her own insider trading case. International media, business, and finance industry observers have analyzed extensively his actions in aiding Rajaratnam. Consensus remains divided on the precise motivators of money, respect, and relationship, with The New York Times asking, 'Why would people who seem to have it all—wealth, prestige, powerful jobs and infinite access to others with the same—risk that, and more, to provide inside information to the Sri Lankan-born billionaire?' Rajaratnam's annual payments were estimated at less than 5% of Kumar's annual income (and just 1-2% excluding a one-time bonus), further raising the question of motivation." ... [This motivation can probably be attributed to the fact that they shared a similar Indian background, and this type of close-nit comradeship is strong and commonplace especially among piers of equal achievers of similar heritage.] (Wikipedia, Anil Kumar)

TOM PETTERS—FRAUD CHARGES

(18) According to Wikipedia, "Thomas Joseph Petters is an American businessman and executive convicted of fraud and imprisoned at the United States Penitentiary, Leavenworth. Petters was the former CEO and chairman of Petters Group Worldwide. Petters resigned his position as CEO on September 29, 2008, amid mounting criminal investigations. He later was convicted for turning Petters Group Worldwide into a $3.65 billion Ponzi scheme and received a fifty year federal sentence. Petters was raised with six siblings in St. Cloud, Minnesota. He worked at the tailor, fur and fabric shop founded by his great-grandfather and operated by his family for over 100 years. In 1973, while still in high school, he started Ear Electronics, a mail-order stereo company aimed at college students. Petters completed only one quarter of college before dropping out to pursue a career. In early 1980s, Petters worked in Colorado as a regional manager at an electronic store chain; when that business went bankrupt, he purchased five of its locations in Colorado and Kansas. In 1988, Petters moved back to Minnesota and founded Amicus Trading, a wholesale brokerage; the name was later changed to The Petters Company, and it marketed consumer merchandise. In 1995, he started Petters Warehouse Direct to sell closeout, overstock and bankrupt company merchandise from a store in Minnetonka, Minnesota, additional locations followed in the Twin Cities and greater Minnesota. In 1998, he went online to sell discounted merchandise through redtag.com, operated by RedTag Inc.; by 2000 he sold his Petters Warehouse Direct stores to focus on his online business, based in Eden Prairie,

Minnesota. He teamed up with direct-mail merchandise company Fingerhut Companies Inc. in 2001 to start a new online store, Redtagbiz.com, which reported sales of $1 billion per year at one point. When Fingerhut's owner, Federated Department Stores, decided to sell or close the company in 2002, Petters, teaming with former Fingerhut chairman Ted Deikel, made an offer to buy the Fingerhut name, customer list, and buildings in St. Cloud, Minnetonka, Plymouth, Minnesota, and Tennessee. The purchase was made in June 2002 and all of Petters operations moved into Fingerhut's former headquarters in Minnetonka. Deikel took over Fingerhut Direct Marketing Inc., which created the catalogs, and Petters took over Fingerhut Fulfillment, based at a St. Cloud distribution center; the new Fingerhut restarted with online and catalog sales in November 2002. In April 2003, The Petters Group, with two minority investors, purchased uBid. The same month, Fingerhut Direct Inc. announced it had obtained a $100 million line of credit to finance inventory and receivables. In 2003, Petters invested in former Democratic State Senator from Minnesota Ted Mondale's Nazca Solutions. Deikel sold his interest in Fingerhut in 2004. In January 2005, Petters Group Worldwide purchased the Polaroid brand for $426 million, with plans to use it on consumer electronics and new technologies. In 2006, Petters Group Worldwide acquired Sun Country Airlines. Petters Group Worldwide became a diverse holding company with 3,200 employees and investments or full ownership in 60 companies, of which it actively managed 20. With offices in North America, South America, Asia, and Europe, it had $2.3 billion in revenue in 2007. Prosecution, conviction and sentencing—The FBI put Petters under investigation for his role in a fraud scheme involving more than $100 million in investments, with estimates ranging up to $3.65 billion. On September 24, 2008, federal investigators raided the Petters headquarters in Minnetonka and searched Tom Petters' Wayzata home. Documents released by the FBI, IRS, and other federal agencies noted that they were seeking evidence of a scheme to lure investors into funding a company based on tens of millions of dollars in purchases and sales that never occurred. The documents noted that a witness associated with Petters and his company came forward with documents and other information, and later wore a hidden microphone and recorded several conversations involving Petters and others who carried out the fraud. The affidavit alleges Petters is caught on tape, repeatedly admitting to the fraud scheme by providing false information to investors, in addition, Petters admits to cheating on his taxes. On

September 29, he resigned as the head of Petters Group Worldwide. On October 3, he was arrested at his home in Wayzata. He was denied bail after prosecutors produced documents that alleged Petters had encouraged another person involved with the case to leave the country, that he regretted turning over his passport, and that he had previously spoken about fleeing the country if the fraudulent scheme was discovered. The U.S. Attorney's office charged him with mail fraud, wire fraud, money laundering and obstruction of justice. The U.S. Attorney staff noted that the government knew nothing about the scheme until Deanna Coleman, vice president of operations for Petters Co., approached them to confess and offered help federal authorities investigate. This led to the prosecution of Robert Dean White, who admitted to being involved in creating false bank statements and other documents that were used to trick investors in what he described as a massive Ponzi scheme. Both individuals made plea bargains with federal prosecutors in exchange for information on how the scheme worked. They noted that, at the direction of Petters, Coleman and White would fabricate documents for Petters and others to use to obtain billions of dollars in loans. The phony records were used as proof that Petters Co. was buying merchandise, generally electronic goods, from two suppliers (who were named as co-defendants). Petters Co. would tell lenders that it was selling the goods through big-box stores and provided purchase orders to substantiate the deals, but the deals were phony and the documents were fakes. Most of the money lent to PCI was secured by promissory notes and sometimes security agreements; the lenders would wire the money to the two suppliers, which would pass it on to Petters Co., less a commission. As more lenders loaned to Petters Co., outstanding loans would be paid off or rolled into new loans from the same lender. Proceeds went to Petters Co. and to Petters himself, and were used to fund other Petters-owned companies, to pay others collaborating in the scheme and, according to court affidavits, for Petters' extravagant lifestyle. Petters' legal troubles led to Sun Country Airlines filing bankruptcy; the airline had been relying on an operating loan from Petters, who owned all the voting shares of Sun Country, to help the low-fare carrier pay its bills during the months of October and November 2008. With the legal troubles surrounding Petters, the airline opted to file for bankruptcy to exempt itself from the legal entanglements of Petters Group Worldwide. The FBI Criminal Complaint identifies First Regional of Century City California as the bank that moved more than $11 billion through an account for Nationwide International Resources Inc. of Los

Angeles. In a separate legal filing in February 2008, more than seven months before the Petters allegations surfaced, the Federal Deposit Insurance Corporation (FDIC) had issued a cease and desist order, which the bank consented to. The order cites First Regional for failing to comply with regulations regarding money laundering with respect to Individual Retirement Accounts and violating rules regarding reporting suspicious activity. During the trial, it emerged that the relationship between Petters and Coleman became 'intimate' for a period of time, ending in 2006. On December 2, 2009, Tom Petters was found guilty in the U.S. District Court in St. Paul, Minnesota on 20 counts of conspiracy, wire and mail fraud. In April 2010, he was sentenced to 50 years in prison for his part in the fraud. Five other employees have pled guilty and are awaiting sentences. Petters' associate and primary fundraiser, Frank Vennes, has been charged with numerous counts of fraud and is awaiting trial." . . . (Wikipedia, Tom Petters)

FANNIE MAE AND FREDDIE MAC—SUBPRIME MORTGAGES

(19) Nick Timiraos et al endorses that, "U.S. Securities regulators accused six former executives at mortgage firms Fannie Mae and Freddie Mack of playing down the risks to investors of the firm's foray into subprime loans. The civil lawsuits filed Friday by the Securities and Exchange Commission in Manhattan federal court, rank among the highest profile crisis-related cases the government has brought. They are also the first cases against the top executives at Fannie and Freddie before their 2008 government takeover, which has cost taxpayers $151 billion. The complaints name as defendants former Freddie Mac Chief Executive Richard Syron and former Fannie Mae CEO Daniel Mudd, who is currently chief executive of Fortress Investment Group LLC. The agency also accused four other high-ranking former executives at Freddie Mac and Fannie Mae. The executives and their lawyers said they would vigorously contest the charges. At the heart of the lawsuits is the government's contention that Fannie and Freddie executives knowingly misled investors about the volumes of risky mortgages that the companies were purchasing as the housing boom turned to bust. 'Fannie Mae and Freddie Mac executives told the world that their subprime exposure was substantially smaller than it really was,' said Robert Khuzami, director of the SEC's Enforcement Division. The lawsuits come as the SEC and other law enforcement agencies face rising political pressure to take more aggressive action against financial

companies over the 2008 crisis. Federal authorities have a mixed record in cases tied to the subprime-mortgage bust, with no major cases having been brought in some of the highest profile blowups, such as the September 2008 bankruptcy of Lehman Brothers Holdings Inc. The SEC, which also has come under criticism from a federal judge questioning the conditions of some major settlements with large financial firms, said it was seeking financial penalties, disgorgement and an order barring the former executives from serving as officers and directors of other companies. 'This is a lawsuit that never should have been brought in the United States of America,' Mr. Mudd said. A statement issued by Mr. Syron, who serves as director of Genzyme Corp, and is an adjunct professor of finance at Boston College, said the case against him is 'without merit.' A Fortress spokesman said the investment firm would undertake a 'thorough review of the matters addressed in the complaint.' The cases brought Friday could be complicated by the fact that there weren't widely accepted definitions about what constituted a subprime or so-called Alt-A mortgage, a category between prime and subprime that allowed for borrowers to provide little or no documentation of their incomes. They seemed likely to turn on whether Fannie and Freddie should have included broader definitions of those loans, such as 'expanded approval' and other new channels created to serve borrowers that normally hadn't been able to obtain conventional mortgages. 'There's no easy way to define subprime, but when you looked at it, it sure looked like they had a lot more subprime than they led people to believe,' said Paul Miller, an analyst who covered the companies for FBR Capital Markets. Fannie and Freddie began experimenting with purchases of subprime mortgages and Alt-A loans in the late 1990's. But the lawsuits provide the latest evidence of how executives sharply boosted those purchases at the worst possible time, in 2006 and 2007, as the housing boom turned to bust. By then Fannie and Freddie were losing market share to Wall Street banks that were assembling big mortgage securitization operations by purchasing large quantities of subprime and other risky loans. But the SEC said that the companies didn't sufficiently warn investors of the risks as they charted that course. In 2007, Mr. Syron and others publicly proclaimed that the single family business through 2006 had 'basically no subprime exposure,' even as executives were warned that more loans had characteristics that made them subprime-like.' The U.S. was forced to take over Fannie and Freddie through a legal process known as conservatorship in 2008, as mounting losses threatened to wipe out their razor-thin capital levels.

The Firms now rely on the U.S. Treasury to remain in business. As part of standard director and officer insurance policies, Fannie and Freddie pay the legal fees of former executives. On Friday, Fannie and Freddie entered into agreements with the securities regulator to avoid civil prosecution. In the civil non-prosecution agreements, the firms said they would accept responsibility for the conduct and not dispute the SEC's allegations, without admitting or denying wrongdoing, the SEC said. As part of those agreements, the government-sponsored firms will cooperate in the regulators' litigation against the former executives, the SEC said. They also agreed to a detailed 'statement of facts' concerning potential shortcomings in disclosures. Neither firm is paying a fine." (Timiraos, 12/17-18/2011)

SUIT OVER MORTGAGE BONDS

(20) Jean Eaglesham et al point out that, "Federal Securities Regulators plan to warn several major banks that they intend to sue them over mortgage-related actions linked to the financial crisis, according to people familiar with the matter. The move would mark a stepped-up regulatory effort to hold Wall Street accountable for its sales of Bonds linked to sub-prime mortgages in 2007 and 2008. At issue is whether the banks misrepresented poor quality of loans pools they bundled and sold to investors, the people said. It isn't clear which firms will receive the formal Securities and Exchange Commission enforcement warnings, known as 'Wells notices.' Banks whose activities are being examined in the civil investigation include Ally Financial Inc., Bank of America Corp., Citigroup Inc., Deutsche Bank AG and Goldman Sachs Group Inc., people familiar with the matter say. Representatives of the banks declined to comment, as did a spokesman for the SEC. In a meeting with reporters last month, Robert Khuzami, the SEC's enforcement chief, said the agency's mortgage-bond investigation was looking for evidence that firms 'failed to disclosed important information when selling these securities.' Mr. Khuzami declined further comment on the investigation. The planned regulatory actions come at a critical juncture. The SEC, Justice Department and state prosecutors are pushing to complete a number of financial-crisis cases by the end of this year, partly to avoid having enforcement action curbed by statutes of limitations, the people said. Some politicians have pressed federal authorities to hold Wall Street firms more accountable for questionable activity during the crisis. President Barack Obama last month set up a new financial-crimes unit to pursue mortgage-securities fraud during

the financial crisis involving federal and state prosecutors and the SEC. This week the SEC hosted a training day for prosecutors and other members of the new unit, the people say. Wall Street firms have defended their actions, saying they couldn't have predicted a market meltdown, that they acted responsibly in chaotic conditions, and that they shouldn't be prosecuted for bad business decisions. For years, financial firms had packaged billions of dollars of bonds by pooling subprime-mortgages into securities. When those mortgages soured, banks and investors suffered losses and write-down on mortgage bonds totaling hundreds of billions of dollars, throwing markets into turmoil and triggering losses that toppled financial giants Bear Sterns Cos., and Lehman Brothers Inc. The multiple pending investigations have the potential to change the way Wall Street operates, according to financial specialists. 'If the SEC is effective in pursuing these cases, the street will take notice,' said Campbell Harvey, finance professor at the Fuqua School of Business at Duke University . . . . The SEC has filed civil lawsuits against a total of 95 firms and individuals related to the financial meltdown; it has at least two additional potential enforcement actions in the works involving mortgage-bond deals, known as collateralized debt obligations or CDOs, the people say . . . . The SEC also is looking at whether any of the banks that received compensation for poor quality loans from the firms that sold them the mortgages passed on these settlement payments to investors, or simply pocketed the money, the people said. On Monday, the SEC is set to face a rare high-profile courtroom battle in a civil case stemming from the financial crisis, when two former Bear Sterns hedge-fund managers go on trial . . . . The most recent SEC mortgage-bond investigation centers on alleged activities similar to those included in civil lawsuits filed against 17 banks in September by the federal agency that oversees Freddie Mac and Fannie Mae. (Eaglesham J. P., 02/09/2012)

SEC UPS GAME TO FIND ROGUE FIRMS

(21) Jean Eaglesham and Steve Eder expresses that, "It is the Security and Exchange Commission's new 'most wanted' list: a chart covered with handwritten notes, yellow highlighter and the names of about 100 hedge funds. The hedge funds have one thing in common: Their performance seems too good to be true, with some trouncing the overall market and others churning out modest results without ever suffering a down month. Some funds on the list stumble but still always outperform rival hedge funds. 'There is serious fraud in this

space, and we have been attacking it,' said Bruce Karpati, co-chair of the SEC's asset management enforcement unit. The hedge-fund chart dominates a corner of his lower Manhattan office. The list is the low-tech product of a high-tech effort by the SEC to crack down on fraud at hedge funds and other investment firms. After the agency failed to detect the $17.3 billion Ponzi scheme by Bernard I. Madoff, who wowed investors with steady returns over several decades, SEC officials decided they needed a way to trawl through performance data and look for red flags that might signal a possible fraud. In 2009, the SEC began developing a computer-powered system that now analyzes monthly returns from thousands of hedge funds. Officials won't say exactly how it works or how much it cost to build, but the agency has announced four civil-fraud lawsuits filed as a result of what it calls the 'aberrational performance initiative.' One hedge fund sued by the SEC reported annual returns of more than 25% by allegedly overvaluing its assets, including Nigerian warrants. A hedge fund of funds received its seemingly great returns by allegedly overriding internal controls on vetting outside funds, causing it to sink investor money into frauds. Encouraged by the results so far, SEC officials are widening the computer-powered scrutiny to mutual funds and private-equity funds. That means data on more than 20,000 funds are being fed into the SEC's computers or soon will be. The enforcement-by-the-numbers machine isn't popular on Wall Street, where some investment managers are worried they might get snagged in an investigation simply because their numbers look too good. SEC enforcement Chief Robert Khuzami rattled some people this year when he suggested that any funds with returns that steadily topped market indexes by 3% could catch the agency's eye. The SEC now says it doesn't see such thresholds. 'There are people out there who have been committing fraud, and we want to get them and get them out of the system,' said Robert Leonard, a partner at law firm Bingham McCutchen LLP who represents hedge funds. 'I'm concerned there probably will be some chilling effect for managers who are knocking the cover of the ball.' Robert Kaplan, the other co-chief of SEC's asset-management enforcement unit, said it isn't so simple. After the SEC's machine spits out the name of a specific hedge-fund, the SEC's 65 person asset-management enforcement unit starts looking for an explanation for the numbers. Some of the hedge funds on the list in Mr. Karpati's office are 'just very good' performers, Mr. Kaplan said, while others seemed suspicious but the activity wasn't clear-cut enough for the SEC to launch an investigation or file a civil lawsuit. Mr. Kaplan wouldn't say how many hedge funds flagged by the 'aberrational performance initiative' wind up as the target of an SEC probe. But the results are encouraging when the SEC tested the computer system in 2009, he said. 'We spotted several cases that we'd recently filed and some others we were already investigating,' Mr. Kaplan said. The system designed partly to detect returns that barely budge when markets are volatile. That might have set off alarms inside the SEC about Mr. Madoff. The SEC has been criticized for failing to identify the Ponzi scheme and for its failure to respond to whistleblowers and their warnings that Mr. Madoff's operations were a fraud. Mr. Madoff's firm collapsed in December 2008, and he is serving a 150-year prison sentence. Among the civil-fraud suits that have resulted from the initiative is one filed against ThinkStrategy Capital Management LLP, which attracted SEC attention partly because it seemed able to defy stock market gravity. In 2008, ThinkStrategy reported a 4.6% return on its Capital Fund-A hedge fund. It was the sixth year in a row that Chetan Kapur, a 36-year-old New Yorker, seemed to have a Midas touch. In contrast, the average hedge fund fell roughly 19% in 2008, with losses in eight of the year's 12 months, according to data from Hedge Fund Research Inc. The SEC alleged in its civil-fraud suit against Mr. Kapur that the 4.6% return figure was faked. The hedge fund actually had a 90% loss in 2008, according to the SEC's lawsuit. The SEC accused Mr. Kapur of continuing to report positive returns for the hedge fund even after it was liquidated and ceased trading, as a way of attracting investors to his other funds. Mr. Kapur also repeatedly inflated his firm's assets under management in investor reports and invented a nonexistent management team, the SEC alleged in its civil-fraud suit. Without admitting or denying wrongdoing, Mr. Kapur agreed to a lifetime ban from the investment industry. A federal court soon will rule on penalties in the case. Mr. Kapur's lawyer, Sam Lieberman of Sadis & Goldberg LLP, said the settlement is a 'favorable development that will allow him to focus on his new business outside the securities industry.' Messrs. Karpati and Kaplan said the data crunching has helped trigger a number of investigations. For private-equity funds, SEC enforcement officials are zooming in on excessive valuations of funds' holdings. Mr. Kaplan said the number crunching on mutual funds has led to an unspecified number of probes 'we're doing that come from similar analysis of outliners." (Eaglesham J. E., 12/27/2011)

SEC EASES REPORTING FOR AUDITS OF TRADING

(22) In the words of Andrew Akerman, "Washington—U.S. regulators are altering plans for a multi-billion-dollar computer system to monitor trades on stock exchanges and other markets to blunt criticism that the project would be expensive and to speed the systems implementation. The Securities and Exchange Commission won't require firms to report comprehensive trading information to the agency in real time as originally proposed, a concession that is welcomed by the financial industry and that experts said would make the system significantly cheaper. Regulators believe that even with a slower system than their original proposal, they would be able to better understand market disruptions such as the May 2010 'flash crash.' 'We're going to be rational here because it's really important to get this basic structure in place sooner than later,' SEC chairman Mary Schapiro said in an interview. The SEC first proposed the system, called the consolidated audit trail, or CAT, about a month after the May 2010 'flash crash' which saw the Dow Jones Industrial Average collapse more than 1,000 points before rebounding. The system is designed so that the agency can reconstruct stock trades but could be expanded to fixed-income, futures and other markets and would make it easier for regulators to identify insider trading. Ms. Schapiro, who could be entering her last year as head of the SEC, said completing the system is one of her highest priorities. The SEC originally estimated its cost at about $4 billion upfront and $2.1 billion annually, borne by the financial industry. [It's not in the least bit surprising that the financial industry would object to this process, since it most certainly would cut into their profits and give them the discomfort that 'big brother' is watching.] SEC officials declined to provide a specific estimate for the scaled-back system. The SEC is expected to adopt a revised framework in the coming months. After that, the Financial Industry Regulatory Authority and exchanges the SEC oversees would have to submit a detailed blueprint, which in turn would be subject to public comment. Patrick Healy, chief executive of **Issuer Advisory Group** LLC a firm that consults with companies about their relationships with exchanges, said the move away from real time is 'significant and the right thing to do. Real time added tremendously to the cost, so this is going to help out a lot,' he said. The SEC has considered devising a CAT system for years, but the idea gathered steam after the agency took five months to explain the flash crash, a delay that led some investors to worry that the regulator had lost control of the markets it oversees. In addition

to detecting trading anomalies, the SEC hopes the audit trail will enable it to more quickly detect manipulative trading activity, such as insider-trading and front-running. The SEC currently relies on data from Finra, which oversees brokerage firms, and twelve exchanges to track the market." (Ackerman, 02/09/2012)

No doubt, there are other episodes similar to those expressed. As long as the opportunities present themselves to business executives, avarice and greed will abound.

INSIDER TRADING PROBE AT SEC—SCANDALOUS

Just when you thought that justice for all investors will be served by the SEC comes this scandalous episode, and who knows if it continues unabated today.

(23) According to Kara Scannell, "Federal prosecutors are investigating whether two Securities and Exchange Commission enforcement lawyers violated insider-trading laws, a potential scandal at an agency normally the pursuer in such cases. A report by the SEC's inspector general described multiple suspicious cases where the lawyers traded the stocks of companies around the time the companies were under investigation. The report concluded the lawyers had violated the agency's internal rules, and the case was taken up by the U.S. attorney's office in Washington D.C., and the Federal Bureau of Investigation. The report didn't identify the employees. One, who the report said had been with the SEC since 1981, is a female staff lawyer, according to people familiar with the matter. The report said the other is a man who works in the enforcement division's chief counsel office, a key position that vets all cases, ensures consistency across the division, and often offers advice to attorneys. The two plus another enforcement lawyer had a "standing lunch" on Monday where they often discussed stocks and financial markets, according to the report it said one made more than 200 trades over two years. Violating internal SEC rules wouldn't necessarily be illegal or criminal. [These branded non-illegal and non-criminal violations, certainly would tempt those who are put in a position of trust. And the question is asked: Who is going to watch the watchman? It makes one wonder how many more incidents like this went un-noticed.] To become illegal insider trading, the transactions would have to involve the use of non-public material information. The report said that the two denied any wrongdoing. Many details of the

alleged activities are unclear, including how much profit, if any, the SEC lawyers might have gained. The FBI investigates many such cases without ever bringing charges. The investigation is another potential hit to the reputation of an agency that is responsible for ensuring the probity of financial markets. It has drawn criticism for missing red flags that could have led it to uncover the giant Bernard Madoff Ponzi scheme. The agency is also under fire for alleged tax regulation of big Wall Street firms and their risky bets prior to the financial crisis. Its future is in question, with Congress and the Obama administration weighing ways to revamp financial regulation. Under Chairman Mary Schapiro, the SEC is seeking to speed up by the enforcement division and enhance the agency's credibility. The agency has taken a particular interest in insider-trading cases on Wall Street in recent years, cracking down on tips and information passed among traders and hedge funds.... In a statement, the SEC said, 'We take seriously even the suggestion that any SEC employee would engage in insider-trading.' It said it is hiring a chief compliance officer and developing a new computer system so it can more easily review securities trading by SEC personnel." (Scannell, 2009)

JAMIE DIMON

(24) As Wikipedia notes, "James 'Jamie' Dimon (born March 13, 1956) is an American business executive. He is the current chairman, president and chief executive officer of JPMorgan Chase, one of the 'big four banks' of the United States, and has served as a Class A director of the Board of Directors of the New York Federal Reserve since January 2007. Dimon was named to Time magazine's 2006, 2008, 2009, and 2011 lists of the world's 100 most influential people. He was also named to Institutional Investor's Best CEOs list in the All-America Executive Team Survey from 2008 through 2011. He was named CEO of the year in 2011. He received a $23 million pay package for fiscal year 2011, more than any other bank CEO in the United States.... On December 31, 2005, he was named chief executive officer of JPMorgan Chase and one year later on December 31, 2006, he was named chairman of the board. In March 2008, he was a board member of the New York Federal Reserve Bank and CEO of JPMorgan and made decisions in connection with the $55 billion loan to JPMorgan to bail out Bear Sterns. Under Dimon's leadership, with the acquisitions during his tenure, JPMorgan Chase has become the leading U.S. Bank in domestic assets under management, market

capitalization value, and publicly traded stock value. JPMorgan Chase is also the No. 1 credit card provider in the U.S. In 2009, Dimon was considered one of "Top Gun CEOs' by Brendan Wood International, an advisory agency. On September 26, 2011, Dimon was involved in a high-profile heated exchange with Mark Carney, the governor of the Bank of Canada, in which Dimon said provisions of the Basel III international financial regulations discriminate against U.S. banks and are 'anti-American'. On May 10, 2012, JPMorgan Chase initiated an emergency conference call to report a loss of at least $2 billion in trades that Dimon said was 'designed to hedge the bank's overall credit risks'. The strategy was, in Dimon's words, 'flawed, complex, poorly reviewed, poorly executed, and poorly monitored'. The episode is being investigated by the Federal Reserve, the SEC, and the FBI. After JPMorgan's $2 billion loss, Paul Krugman criticized Dimon as the point man in Wall Street's fight to delay, water down and/or repeals financial reform. He has been particularly vocal in his opposition to the so-called Volker Rule, which would prevent banks with government-guaranteed deposits from engaging in 'proprietary trading', basically speculating with depositors' money. Just trust us, the JPMorgan chief has in fact been saying; everything's under control. Apparently not . . . . Federal TARP Funds—As head of JPMorgan Chase, Dimon oversaw the transfer of $25 billion in funds from the U.S. Treasury Department to the bank on October 28, 2008, under the Troubled Asset Relief Program (TARP). This was the fifth largest amount transferred under section A of TARP to help troubled assets related to residential mortgages. It has been widely reported that JPMorgan Chase was in much better financial shape than other banks and did not need TARP funds but accepted the funds because the government did not want to single out only the banks with capital issues. [What a load of crap! Taxpayers' money was eagerly accepted by these Banks and other institutions that did not need it, so that huge bonuses could be given to their executives. Taxpayers' mortgages were under water and while they struggled, the same banks refused to give refinancing and modifications to the populace.] JPMorgan Chase advertised in February 2009 that it would be using its capital-base monetary strength to acquire new businesses. By February 2009, the U.S. government had not moved forward in enforcing TARP's intent of funding JPMorgan Chase with $25 billion. In face of the government's lack of action, Dimon was quoted during the week of February 1, 2009, as saying; JPMorgan would be fine if we stopped talking about the damn nationalization of banks. We've got plenty of capital. To policymakers, I say where were they? . . . They approved all these banks. Now they are beating up on everyone, saying look at these mistakes, and we are going to come and fix it. JPMorgan Chase was arguably the healthiest of the nine largest U.S. banks and did not need to take TARP funds. In order to encourage smaller banks with troubled assets to accept this money, Treasury Secretary Henry Paulson allegedly coerced the CEOs of the nine largest banks to accept TARP money under short notice. JPMorgan Chase was also the first of the largest banks to repay the TARP money. Dimon is a democrat and worked in Barack Obama's adopted hometown of Chicago. After Obama won the 2008 presidential election, there was speculation that Dimon would serve in the Obama Administration as Secretary of the Treasury. Obama eventually named the president of the Federal Reserve Bank of New York, Timothy Geithner, to the position. Following the acquisition of Washington Mutual by JPMorgan Chase, Obama commented on Dimon's handling of the real-estate crash, credit crisis, and the banking collapse affecting corporations nationwide, including major financial institutions like Bank of America, Citibank, and Wachovia: You know, keep in mind, though there are a lot of banks that are actually pretty well managed, JPMorgan being a good example, Jamie Dimon, the CEO there, I don't think should be punished for doing a pretty good job managing an enormous portfolio. Dimon is influential in the Obama White House with close ties to some there, including former Chief of Staff Rahm Emanuel. Dimon is one of three CEOs—along with Lloyd Blankfein and Vikram Pandit—said by the Associated Press to have liberal access to Treasury Secretary Timothy Geithner. Nonetheless, Dimon has often publicly disagreed with some of Obama's policies. On the May 15, 2012, episode of ABC's 'The View', Obama responded to a question from Whoopi Goldberg regarding JPMorgan Chase's recently publicized $2 billion trading losses by defending Dimon against allegations of irresponsibility, saying, 'first of all, JPMorgan is one of the best managed banks there is. Jamie Dimon, the head of it, is one of the smartest bankers we've got', but added, 'it's going to be investigated". (Wikipedia, Jamie Dimon, 2012)

[As of today, July 16, 2012, it was mentioned on national television that the JPMorgan Chase Scandal was approaching $5.8 billion and counting. And according to reliable sources, Jamie Dimon had to go because he had lost the trust of regulators].

CHAPTER FIVE

MAJOR INVESTIGATION OF SCANDAL AT AMEX

CORNERSTONE PLAQUE

In the words of Susan P. Shapiro, "Beginning in 1958, reports refer to a 'Special Investigations Unit' in the Division of Trading and Exchanges, called the

'Office of Special Investigations' (1961), 'Branch of Special Investigations, Trial and Enforcement' (1961), and 'Office of Enforcement' (1962) in subsequent years. This unit was involved in some special investigations of boiler-room operations in the New York area, followed by a major investigation of a scandal that erupted at the American Stock Exchange (AMEX) in the late 1950's and 1960's. It became clear from these investigative efforts that the SEC lacked the capacity for quick response to pressing matters, offences of national scope, or offences of depth, complexity, and breadth that were not being picked up by the regional offices. The home office was the natural setting for developing such an investigative capacity; the investigation of the AMEX scandal provided the impetus. [This is just one of quite a few scandals that continued at the Amex until their demise. There is nothing new in the present world of trading improprieties. This has occurred in years gone by and will continue beyond present-day illicit activities; not only on the AMEX, but on all Stock Exchanges and Brokerage Houses, which have all had their share of scandals.]

… Shortly thereafter, home office personnel were involved in the preparation of the 'Special Study of the Securities Markets,' a massive investigation of the adequacy of the national securities exchanges and associations in protecting investors, ordered by Congress in September 1961 and completed in mid-1963. A staff of about sixty-five persons was assembled for the special study. Many of them were subsequently available for enforcement work. By many accounts, the completion of the study marked the emergence of the home office as a significant contributor to SEC enforcement". (Shapiro, Wayward Capitalists, 1984), 138-140

A PROPOSITION REVEALED ON A MERGER

The Capital Trading Exchange (CTE) by this time was now defunct due to the more aggressive competitive trading practices of its rivals. Next was the proposed takeover of the American Stock Exchange (AMEX) by another competitor—the National Association of Securities Dealers (NASD).

Initially, this proposal caused much consternation for the membership of the American Stock Exchange, since the membership was not yet aware of secret talks between the two Stock Exchanges for a merger. On Wednesday, March 11, 1998; there was a news leak to The Wall Street Journal and The New York Times that secret talks were held for a merger acquisition by the NASD for the American Stock Exchange. As is well known, nothing is hidden for long from the diligent and competitive reporters of American media.

On Thursday, March 12, 1998, the headlines were all about the proposed merger. Until then, hardly anyone employed at the AMEX including the Floor Brokers paid much attention to the news, since no Amex Official communicated that this was a possibility or in the works. Amex Officials were so embarrassed by the news leak that later on that day, a circular was hurriedly sent out to inform every one of the proposed merger talks held between the Governors of the Amex and Officials of the NASD. The talks were so secretive that none of the staff, the brokers and certain high-profile Floor Officials knew about the secret talks. The circular that hit the Trading Floor, was sent out to save face and put up a defense for their secrecy. The explanation given was that: (1) The NASD approached the AMEX and not the other way around. (2) That the NASD did so because they saw the many advantages of adding an order-driven auction market to their quote-driven dealer market. (3) The NASD wished to extend their product offerings by including Options trading, and that a membership meeting will be held at 4:30 p.m.in the Boardroom on March 12, and a review of the proposal to be held on the morning of March 13, 1998.

The circular that was sent out on March 12, 1998 was addressed to the 'All Floor Members" so other Staff members of the Amex were not fully aware of what was about to take place. Friday, March 13, 1988, as employees of the Amex approached the Amex to report for duty, they were greeted with the site of mobile television vehicles lining both sides of the street in front of 86 Trinity Place, Downtown Manhattan. When those employees got inside from the initial surprise of the media coverage, the trading floor was alive with chatter about the proposed merger. Many Members were dissatisfied with the details of the proposal, and had a lot of unanswered questions. The Amex members complained that by conceding to the merger, it raised concerns that the Amex's auction market and the NASDAQ's electronic system combined will mean less business on the floor causing the value of their seats to drop. In an attempt to quell opposition to the proposal, a very prominent Washington DC official who was at the time one of the Governors of the Amex, was brought in on the trading floor of the Red-Room at the Intel Options crowd to further explain and encourage passage of the proposed merger.

March 18, 1998, The American Stock Exchange announced an agreement in principle for the historic merger with the National Association of Securities Dealers (NASD). It was proposed that the Amex would remain a separate specialist-based auction market, while at the same time to operate and benefit from the technology of the NASD. The NASDAQ Stock Market would be a sister subsidiary to the wholly owned Amex subsidiary, both operating under the NASD. Seat owners would be allowed to retain their rights to trading and the right to lease their seats to others. The NASD was to provide $30 million for a seat stabilization program for regular seat owners. It was understood that the proposal was subject to a vote by the membership according to the Amex by-laws. The Board of Governors of the American Stock Exchange approved a set of basic terms for the proposed transaction. Many negotiations had to be worked out in order to have a definitive agreement. According to conversations on the trading floor, the Amex membership had to approve the deal by a two-thirds majority vote. The NASD would provide $110 million for the enhancement of leading edge technology and a further $58 million for restructuring. Options Trading, which was the income backbone of the Amex was to remain basically the same in market structure, and it did. And there were no substantial changes to Equity Trading. October 30, 1998—the acquisition was completed after the needed two-third majority vote by the Amex membership and regulatory approval. Amex Inc., according to reliable sources, transferred all of its assets and liabilities to Amex LLC.

CREATING A GLOBAL MARKET

NASD—MANHATTAN, N.Y.

March 18, 1998—The National Association of Securities Dealers (NASD) and the American Stock Exchange (AMEX) reached a tentative agreement between both boards of governors for an agreement to merge, subject of course to the approval by the members of the Amex. This merger would also need the scrutiny and approval of the SEC. The merger would allow the NASDAQ and the AMEX to combine their technology, expertise and executions to court investors worldwide. Though the two entities would be under the umbrella of the NASD, they would be allowed to operate independently. This was a fight for survival by both the AMEX and the NASDAQ.

The merger also took on the premise that it would provide a more efficient pricing system, better and faster auction executions through automated electronic limit order books, and less transaction fees. This association between the two exchanges was the first attempt of creating a "global market of markets" by connecting through a global network of computers for investors around the world, facilitating price competitiveness. The American Stock Exchange was at the time the only marketplace in the United States for both equities and options, while the NASD was the largest securities industry SRO in the United States.

THE NASD DEAL

> Amy Feldman asserts that, "Among the deal's highlights: $110 million would be allocated for updated technology over five years; $30 million for marketing over two years, and $40 million to safeguard members against sliding seat prices—a 'seat stabilization' expense that is slated to increase to $50 million over time. But there would be hefty severance and personnel costs of up to $20 million. Additionally, the Amex would owe the National Association of Securities Dealers $1 million if the deal is not completed by year-end and $3.5 million if the deal is derailed permanently. Just two months ago, Syron and his counterpart at the NASD, Frank Zarb, reached the historic agreement to combine their respective organizations into a more powerful operation intended to aggressively compete with the New York Stock Exchange. But the deal has stirred up plenty of opposition among Amex members, especially with absentee owners who rent their seats. Paul Liang, a Chicago-based investor who owns 17 Amex seats, has circulated letters opposing the deal, and a group of absentee owners has even begun calling for the ouster of the exchange's management. Some members fear the prices of their seats will decline from the $480,000 level of February, while others are angry that they will lose clout in the merger without getting a big payout. 'The members don't want this thing,' said seat-holder Warren Schwartz. 'I want the members to put up an ad in the paper to say, 'Get rid of these bums.' In a continuing attempt to woo members, Amex officials are slated to meet tomorrow with long-time members and a second presentation is

slated for Florida, home of many absentee seat-holders. If the merger is approved, the American Stock Exchange might move out of its Trinity Place building, where it has had its headquarters for 77 years." [That move would have cost an enormous amount of money, which neither of the two exchanges could have afforded.] (Amex members getting numbers on NASD deal, 1998)

DISAPPOINTMENT AND DISPLEASURE

After a two year period of the marriage between the NASDAQ and the AMEX, there was much malcontent. The relationship soured and the many concerns of the Amex Traders that were expressed on the morning of March 13, 1998; reverberated once more, shaking the foundations of the merger that was supposed to create a "market of markets".

The concerns back in March of 1998, was that all the grandiose talks and the meetings by Amex Board of Governors and other officials; stating that the Amex stand to gain tremendously from increased volume, never panned out. The concerns of the seat owners (membership) at that time, was that the combination of the Amex' auction market and the NASDAQ electronic system would mean less business on the Amex Trading Floor, causing the value of seats to decline; and so it did, with the price of seats falling from about $650,000 to about $300,000 each for the regular (equity-trader) membership. The "Option Principal Member" (OPM) seats which allowed traders to trade only options were generally much cheaper. With the noted Amex Governor's influence and the cunning of Frank Zarb and the Amex officials, after a series of meetings—the deal went through.

The traders on the Amex, nevertheless, submitted with reservations in tow. By the year 2000, nerves were frayed, and the Amex traders threatened to bring a law-suit against the NASD. The large number of listings that were supposed to come to the floor of the Amex never materialized. In fact, the Amex was seeing a drop in equity listings—among them—the big players like Intel, Cablevision Systems, Dell, Hasbro, Viacom and others.

There was some talk between brokers on the Amex trading floor, about lowering the listing standards for small-cap companies—but that was just desperate wishful thinking on the part of financially and emotionally hurt Amex seat owners. With that in mind, "how low can you go"? The Amex already had in place a "low listing standard" for emerging companies, in order to ramp up the competition with other exchanges. Any further lowering of the listing-standards would have had the Amex taking on the characteristics of a crack-cocaine house.

It is amazing how three men, Salvatore Sodano, Frank Zarb and Richard F. Syron managed to influence the entire membership of the Amex into believing that they would create a Shangri-La for them by sending more companies to list on the Amex.

Surely these men (the membership) of stock market knowledge and experience had to know that the NASDAQ cannot tell companies which exchange to list their companies on. Those companies will make their decisions based on the desire for more exposure and the ability to meet the listing requirements of the appropriate Stock Exchange.

THE PARTING OF THE WAVES

After all that was said and done, the Amex and the NASD reached the conclusion, that it was time for the parting of the waves. The National Association of Securities Dealers relinquished the Amex, sometime in 2001. In preparation of an ultimate decision to sell the American Stock Exchange to another rival exchange; the decision makers terminated a sizeable number of its staff in November of 2002. Needless to say that it was the first public reveal of staff being cut. All the other cuts before that were done quietly without public fanfare. Even members of the junior staff for some years saw the writing on the wall of a slowly dying Amex, desperately holding on to life support.

Prior to that termination of staff in November 2002, primarily, only the junior staff felt the heat, while the top-heavy administrative staff enjoyed bigger salaries and larger year-end bonuses—which reinforced the Amex's financial shortfall. The Amex Big-wigs or "suits" as they were called, enjoyed their self-aggrandizement at the expense of junior staff, while reinforcing that listing companies should not give gifts at Christmas time, of more than one hundred dollars to any Amex trading floor staff that was assigned to work with them.

Meanwhile, there was talk on the Amex Trading Floor of several interested buyers for the Amex's Art Deco Building, which started out as the "Curb Market". Over the years the American Stock Exchange sought to improve and upgrade their trading floor with Quotron and Instinet Technology, but apparently, not fast enough to compete with other exchanges. As a result, their competitors were always able to front-run and improve their spreads, so as to grab the hog of the competition.

The American Stock Exchange will always be remembered by a number of trading floor staff and by some of the office staff for the unscrupulous deeds of the Iron Lady. She sought relentlessly to circumvent the Amex staff form receiving "buyouts", using lame excuses to fire her office staff, and fought with attorneys to try and disenfranchise a few of the Amex staff from their lawfully earned "retirement packages". Thanks to NYSE Euronext, retirees from the American Stock Exchange can breathe easy—enjoying good medical coverage at nominal prices, free "Will Preparation Services" and a "Retiree Life Insurance Plan".

PHILADELPHIA EXCHANGE TO MERGE WITH NASDAQ & AMEX

Greg Ip claims that, "The Securities Exchange landscape changed again as the Philadelphia Stock Exchange, the country's oldest, agreed to join the American Stock Exchange and the Nasdaq Stock Market's parent in their 'market of markets.' After several months of talks with both the Amex and the Chicago Board of Options Exchange, the Philadelphia Exchange announced an agreement in principle to join with the Amex and the National Association of Securities Dealers operator of NASDAQ, which have themselves already agreed to merge. In the process, Philadelphia rejected a competing proposal by the CBOE made public last week. The AMEX-NASD merger is to be voted on by Amex members June 25, 1998. When either agreement goes through, it would be the first time in about 30 years that a U.S. Stock Exchange has merged into another marketplace. The new agreement, which was expected, caps a tumultuous and difficult two years for the Philadelphia Exchange, including a series of governance controversies and the departures of two chief executive officers. Now the Exchange is giving up its independence after 208 years in business. 'Through this combination, we will have the resources, state-of-the-art technologies and management strength to achieve a more efficient, transparent and low-cost market structure,' said John F. Wallace, acting chairman of the Philadelphia Stock Exchange. The agreement 'shows the power of this AMEX/NASD combination,' said Richard Syron, chairman and chief executive officer of the Amex. Amex's attractiveness as a merger partner to Philadelphia was enhanced by the expected combination with the NASD, and its 'ongoing technology commitment which translates directly to competitiveness in this business. Our partnership with the NASD is what enables this.' Richard Ketchum, chief operating officer of the NASD, said the agreement builds on the NASD's strategy 'to provide under one tent the most efficient, low cost and effective dealer, auction and options market in the U.S., if not the world.' Under the agreement in principle the Philadelphia exchange will continue to operate its floor in Philadelphia for five years. [However, the Amex was insistent that a couple of options and Brokers from the Philadelphia exchange should start moving to the Amex to test the waters, which they did. The Brokers and the officials of the Philadelphia exchange grew disenchanted and for whatever other reasons which were known only to officials of both exchanges; the Brokers and their options moved back to the Philadelphia Exchange.] But Philadelphia members, should they choose, could move to New York and work there in as few as three years. In exchange for their seats, Philadelphia members will receive permits to trade their current securities exclusively for the five-year transition period, plus newly developed securities. For the subsequent seven years, both Amex and Philadelphia members could trade the Philadelphia securities, while Philadelphia members would be permitted to trade a restricted volume of Amex products. [Is this where the disagreements began, along with too many directives?] After twelve years, Philadelphia members would be expected to buy Amex seats to keep trading. The Amex will as soon as possible start providing options-trading technology to Philadelphia. Indeed, spreading the high and rising cost of technology over more trading volume has been a key driver of both mergers. Philadelphia's prized option on Dell Computer stock will be moved as soon as possible to the Amex—possibly within days. The current specialists and market makers from Philadelphia would retain the exclusive right to trade Dell. That appears aimed at minimizing the likelihood that the CBOE will 'dual-list' the option and compete for orders in that lucrative security. The merger is still subject to the approval of a definitive agreement by the boards of governors of each organization, the Amex and Philadelphia Stock Exchange memberships and the appropriate regulatory authorities, including the Securities and Exchange Commission. The boards of the NASD and the Amex approved the agreement late Monday. Mr. Syron said the offer to Philadelphia stands even if Amex members don't approve their merger with NASD. But he said yesterday's announcement will make the Amex-NASD merger even more attractive to Amex members. Additional terms will be defined in the coming weeks, the organizations said in a joint news release. The largest unresolved issue appears to be the role of Philadelphia's equity floor. While the floor—which accounts for up to about one-sixth of Philadelphia's 505 members—is included in the merger, its exact function in the new entity has yet to be determined. Mr. Wallace raised the prospect with Philadelphia members yesterday that the equity floor, which trades primarily New York Stock Exchange listed stocks, could remain much as it is for 20 years, said a person who attended the meeting. That, however, is not part of the formal agreement. The deal will reduce the number of options markets in the U.S. to three from four, and the Amex would become a closer second to the CBOE in terms of market share. In the first quarter of the year, the CBOE had 51% of national market share in stock and stock-index option trading volume, compared the Amex's 23%, the San Francisco's based Pacific Exchange's 15%, and Philadelphia's10%. The merger would thus lift Amex's share to 33%. In stock options only, Amex would go to 38% from 28%, just behind the CBOE's 43%. William Brodsky, CBOE chairman and chief executive officer, said yesterday that Philadelphia's decision is 'a victory for investors' CBOE's proposal had been seen as weaker because it called for a shorter transition period, a more restrictive trading permit and offered no solution for the equity floor. 'We're not putting a counteroffer on the table,' Mr. Brodsky said, adding that Amex had a strong advantage from the start in its closer proximity to Philadelphia. 'I don't look at this as being that dramatic a competitive threat,' he said. A person close to the Philadelphia exchange said the Amex and NASD will try to find jobs for as many of Philadelphia's displaced employees in their merged operations as possible. The merger will likely need approval from two-thirds of Philadelphia's membership. A proposed merger with CBOE failed to even come to a vote in 1993 amid infighting among the membership. Arnold Staloff, head of Bloom Staloff Corp., which operates on Philadelphia's stock-option and currency-options floors, said, 'As a member that's been against combining with exchanges in the past, I believe the deal as proposed is an excellent proposal and should be readily adopted by the membership.' (Ip, 06-10-1998)

NASD AND THE NYSE FUED OVER AMEX

According to Deborah Lohse, "At a 1996 meeting of the American Association of Individual Investors in New York, a session leader answered a question about the Nasdaq Stock Market with a casual explanation: "Well! You know the NASDAQ market is crooked.' That attitude was extreme but understandable, given that the Justice Department in 1996 censured traders for allegedly rigging prices to their own advantage, and the Securities and Exchange Commission rebuked Nasdaq's owner and self-regulator, the National Association of Securities Dealers, for failing to adequately police their activity. That view of NASDAQ also left some observers wondering who in his right mind would want the job then being vacated by the retiring NASD chief executive, Joseph Hardiman. They figured the NASD would have to spend years in the penalty box rebuilding the trust of investors and the SEC, with the only real power residing with the newly enlarged regulatory unit run by longtime regulator Mary Schapiro. But that was before Frank G. Zarb came on the scene. The 63-year-old former Ford-administration energy czar and Smith Barney executive took the helm of the NASD in February 1997, becoming the first NASD chief ever to take on all three titles of chairman, president and CEO. Wielding those powers with zeal and energy, he has transferred NASDAQ, keeping the NASD's regulatory pressure at full throttle, challenging head-on the predominance of the New York Stock Exchange under its equally competitive CEO, Richard Grasso, and, in some cases, barreling over the wishes of his membership to leave much of their old way of life intact. 'It seemed to me, as I looked at the landscape, that every part of the industry had gone through radical change . . . except the business of exchanging stocks,' Mr. Zarb says. His latest and boldest move was the announcement last month that the NASD had reached an agreement to acquire the American Stock Exchange, spending more than $200 million over the next several years to improve the Amex's technology and marketing to compensate Amex seat holders for any declines in their seat values. (The Big Board's Mr. Grasso, for his part, says the exchange is keeping a close eye on the competitive challenge from the Nasdaq-Amex marriage.) Mr. Zarb says his vision for Nasdaq is to give investors a choice of trading—a 'market of markets' using either traditional dealers or high-speed electronic systems that maximize the chance that limit orders, or orders to buy and sell at a specified price, are exposed to the full range of possible matching orders. At the same, time he wants to give companies a choice of where to trade their shares, either on the auction market of Amex where one specialist largely handles each stock, or on the dealer market, where multiple market makers compete to offer the best price for a stock. Not the least of his aims, of course, is to challenge the pre-eminence of the Big Board No. 1 U.S. market and model for auction markets. 'I like the idea of starting with a company that was considered No. 2' and building a team that has the goal to become No. 1,' Mr. Zarb says. He isn't above being downright flashy in his challenge to the Big Board. In a bid to polish Nasdaq's brand image, Mr. Zarb is considering moving part of its marketing operations to a corner of the city's renovated Times Square neighborhood, around 43rd Street and Broadway, where Nasdaq's glitzy 55-by-11-foot Market Site 'wall' of 100 video screens would be easily visible to throngs of tourists and New Yorkers. The Market Site currently is housed in relative obscurity on the ninth floor of an older building in lower Manhattan, though it has gotten some play on television in recent months. 'We don't have a floor where CNN can watch us ring a bell every night,' Mr. Zarb says. Contrasting NASDAQ's computerized system with the human beehive of activity that marks the Big Board's trading floor. Details are still being worked out, he says, adding that he is still trying to finesse the deal without enlarging NASDAQs well-padded marketing budget. Mr. Zarb says many of the changes he has made during the past year were blue-printed in his mind when he took the job. A merger between the NASD and the Amex, for instance, has been percolating for years without results. 'The conventional wisdom was that a merger of two exchanges was too hard, but the nice thing about Frank is he doesn't listen to conventional wisdom.' says Richard Ketchum, the NASD's chief operating officer, whom Mr. Zarb promoted to president as well. A few months into his new job in the summer of 1997, Mr. Zarb met with Richard Syron, the Amex's chairman, and hammered out an idea for a merger that would have listed all NASDAQ and Amex stocks on both markets, with specialists opening the stocks in the morning and NASDAQ market makers free to post quotes for the stocks. The plan hit insurmountable obstacles, such as how to ensure an orderly opening and how market makers and specialists would relate to one another. The recently approved merger, which will keep NASDAQ and Amex as distinct markets with different trading structures, was hatched at a meeting over drinks between Mr. Zarb and Mr. Syron while the two were attending a Securities Industry Association meeting in Boca Raton, Fla., in November, Mr. Zarb says. While it took months to work out the merger, Mr. Zarb moved much faster on other items. Early in his tenure, according to Ms. Schapiro, the president of NASD Regulation, she and Mr. Zarb 'were sitting around the office one day,' with other NASD executives, and Frank asked, 'What's something you think has the potential to jump up and bite us?' 'We all said the micro-cap market' Ms. Schapiro recalls. Mr. Zarb immediately supported making changes in listing standards. 'That surprised me a little bit' Ms. Schapiro says. 'I'm not sure I expected somebody from the industry to have such a regulatory approach.' Mr. Zarb says the master plan with which he joined NASD is largely in place, 'I guess the vision part is 80% there. The hard part is the doing part,' he says. He has a three year contract, ending in February 2000, which is subject to board renewal. The remaining 20% of his vision, Mr. Zarb says, is to team up with some other international exchange, either through a joint venture or a merger, to 'link the pools of liquidity around the world.' He wants to make it easier for the NASDAQ market makers to invest in non-U.S. issues and for overseas traders to 'create a price discovery mechanism after our markets close.' He says that right now traders in Germany would be reluctant to trade a NASDAQ security without NASDAQ being open, because it's too risky to set prices in a vacuum. He envisions, perhaps as much as a decade from now, having a full presence of NASDAQ market makers in other markets, effectively creating round-the-clock trading. 'One of the things we have never gotten to is extending the trading day,' Mr. Zarb says. Already, NASDAQ plans to announce a deal soon with the Hong Kong market to display quotes and other data on Hong Kong-listed stocks through NASDAQ's web site. People close to the NASD say a joint venture of some sort ultimately may be worked out with the exchange in Hong Kong, which trades about 725 stocks, or in Frankfurt, where 1,000 stocks trade. Mr. Zarb walks a tightrope sometimes, as many changes he is overseeing require him to bulldoze over the objections of some of his own membership. For example, under his guidance, NASDAQ is closer than ever to implementing a long-discussed 'central limit-order-book' that will showcase customer orders to trade at specific prices on NASDAQ's trading system. But some NASDAQ traders complain the book puts NASDAQ in direct competition with them by allowing such orders to execute against one another without first giving market makers a crack at them. 'Philosophically, I have a problem with any regulator being a competitor in the market,' an official at one large market-making firm says. Another change, which has infuriated some of Mr. Zarb's members, is a preliminary plan to enter into an equity-sharing agreement with a new institutional-trading system, OptiMark. OptiMark, which isn't yet operational, ultimately will encourage mutual-fund trading desks to bypass market makers and enter their trading preferences into a black-box system, where a complex algorithmic system will match them up against other orders in the system, or in NASDAQ's planned new limit order book. Dow Jones & Co., the publisher of the Wall Street Journal, has a minority stake in OptiMark. Some dealers resent NASDAQs giving prominence and backing to an untested alternative trading system that will compete directly with NASD members. They say other NASD members one day may want to compete with the technology, but NASDAQ already will have given its imprimatur to OptiMark. But Alfred Berkeley, the president of NASDAQ, says such systems are inevitable. 'Let's be the leader in bringing these new technologies into our market, even though we know these are contentious issues. It's better to have them in our market,' he says, than draining market share from afar." (Lohse, 1998)

THE AMEX AS CHEAP STREET

There was a brilliant article in a New York newspaper so accurately written and so compelling, but could not be reprinted due to "permission denied" by the rights-holder. The article irked Officials of the Amex so much, that an angry reply was sent from Corporate Communications to that newspaper on February 25, 2003. Truth be told—the American Stock Exchange in its attempt to up the ante to compete with other exchanges lowered the listing requirements, and operated like a hooker in a crack-house.

OFFICE ENTRANCE
86 TRINITY PLACE, N.Y. NY.

The obvious slashing of the listing standards by the American Stock Exchange officials, accomplished the opposite to what the head-honchos with their fat salaries and bonuses foolishly expected. Instead of attracting classic buoyant companies that would cause the AMEX to rise to the top of the crop, the AMEX took a hurried dive into the trash-bin. Eventually those listed stocks were considered by SEC standards, to be rated as "penny-stocks". To scrounge even lower, option derivatives with strike prices of 2.5 and 5 were established to attempt to bring in a few more pennies. Shameful!

THE AMEX AS A COMPETITIVE EXCHANGE (SRO)

Officials of the Amex always sought to establish the Amex as the premier marketplace of the nation, by way of public advertising and portraying itself as an Exchange with a squeaky clean image. Their major concern was to keep all negative complaints, investigations and so-called resolutions mum from the public. They invited the Emerging Companies with minimum requirements to list their companies on the Amex, and swayed the public investors to come on board; boasting about how many companies they had listed each month, some of which got "delisted" after a short period of trading.

NYSE Euronext TO ACQUIRE AMEX

Wikipedia states that, "On January 17, 2008, NYSE Euronext announced it would acquire the American Stock Exchange for $260 million in stock. On October 1, 2008, NYSE Euronext completed acquisition of the American Stock Exchange. Before the closing of the acquisition, NYSE Euronext announced that the Exchange would be integrated with the Alternext European small-cap exchange and renamed the NYSE Alternext U.S. In March 2009, NYSE Alternext U.S. was changed to NYSE Amex Equities." (Wikipedia, American Stock Exchange)

OFFICE ENTRANCE
NYSE EURONEXT, N.Y.

Wikipedia concludes that, "Due to the apparent moves by the NASDAQ to acquire the London Exchange; NYSE Group bid Euros 8 billion in cash and shares for Euronext on May 22, 2006, outbidding a rival offer for the European Stock Exchange operator from Germany's Deutsche Borse, the German Stock Market. Contrary to statements that it would not raise its bid, on May 23, 2006, Deutsche Borse unveiled a merger bid for Euronext, valuing the pan-European exchange at U.S.$ 11 billion (Euros 8.6 billion), Euros 600 million over NYSE Group's initial bid. Despite this, NYSE Group and Euronext penned a merger agreement, subject to shareholder vote and regulatory approval. The initial regulatory response by the U.S. Securities and Exchange Commission chief Christopher Cox (who was coordinating heavily with European counterparts) was positive, with an expected approval by the end of 2007. The new firm tentatively dubbed NYSE Euronext, would be headquartered in New York City, with European operations and its trading platform run out of Paris. NYSE CEO John Thain, who would head NYSE Euronext, intends to use the combination to form the world's first global stock market, with continuous trading of stocks and derivatives over a 21-hour time span. In addition the two exchanges hoped to add Borsa Italiana (the Milan Stock Exchange) into the grouping. On June 23, 2007, the Borsa Italiana was however sold to the London Stock Exchange. Deutsche Borse dropped out of the bidding for Euronext on November 15, 2006, removing the last major hurdle for the NYSE Euronext transaction. A run-up of NYSE Group's stock price in late 2006 made the offering far more attractive to Euronext's shareholders. On December 19, 2006, Euronext shareholders approved the transaction by a 98.2 % margin. The remainder voted in favor of the Deutsche Borse offer. Jean-Francois Theodore, the Chief Executive Officer of Euronext, stated that they expected the transaction to close within three or four months. Some of the regulatory agencies with jurisdiction over the merger had already given approval. NYSE Group shareholders gave their approval on December 20, 2006. The NYSE consummated its U.S. $11 billion takeover of Paris-based exchange operator Euronext NV at ceremonies in the U.S. and Europe on April 4, 2007.

NYSE Euronext operates and holds stake in: the New York Stock Exchange (NYSE), Euronext, NYSE Liffe, NYSE Arca, NYSE Arca Europe, NYSE Alternext, NYSE Amex, NYSE Liffe US, LLC (NYSE Liffe US), NYSE Technologies, Inc. (NYSE Technologies), Easy Next, Blue Next, Free Market (Marche' Libre), Smart Pool, and NYSE BondMatch.

NYSE EURONEXT, N.Y.

... On May 4, 2010, NYSE Euronext and the Financial Industry Regulatory Authority (FINRA) announced that FINRA would assume responsibility for performing the market surveillance and enforcement functions originally conducted by NYSE Regulation. The agreement was subject to review by the Securities and Exchange Commission and completed by the end of June, 2010.

Under the agreement announced, FINRA assumed regulatory functions for NYSE Euronext's U.S. equities and options markets—the New York Stock Exchange, NYSE Arca and NYSE Amex. FINRA currently provides regulatory services to the NASDAQ Stock Market, NASDAQ Options Market, NASDAQ OMX Philadelphia, NASDAQ OMX Boston, The BATS Exchange and the International Securities Exchange.

NYSE Euronext, through its subsidiary NYSE Regulation, remains ultimately responsible for overseeing FINRA's performance of regulatory services for the NYSE markets. The agreement involved approximately 225 staff, most of who will be transferred to FINRA. (Wikipedia, NYSE Euronext, Inc.)

BIBLIOGRAPHY

(n.d.).

Ackerman, A. (02/09/2012). SEC Eases Reporting for Audits of Trading. *The Wall Street Journal*, C3.

Barrett, D. C. (11/17/2011). U.S. Levels Subpoenas In Probe of MF Global. *The Wall Street Journal*, C1—C2.

Bray, C. (Tuesday, November 8, 2011). Citigroup Settlement 'Fair,' SEC Tells Court. *Wall Street Journal*, C3.

Chernova, Y. (2011). Dark Times Fall on Solar Sector. *The Wall Street Journal*, B1-B2.

Eaglesham, J. E. (12/27/2011). SEC Ups Game to Find Rogue Firms. *The Wall Street Journal*, C1-C5.

Eaglesham, J. P. (02/09/2012). Banks to Face Lawsuit by U.S. *The Wall Street Journal*, C1-C2.

Eaglesham, S. E. (Friday, December 23, 2011). Falcone Rejects an Offer By SEC. *The Wall Street Journal*, C1-C2.

Favole, J. A. (April 5, 2012). Ban On Insider Trading By Congress Becomes Law. *The Wall Street Journal*, A6.

Feldman, A. (1998, May 19). *Amex members getting numbers on NASD deal*. Retrieved June 6, 2012, from NY Daily News: http://articles.nydailynews.com/1998-05-19/news/18069537_1_american-stock-exchange-a . . .

Hilzenrath, D. S. (2011, October 13). *Raj Rajaratnam, hedge fund billionaire, gets 11-year sentence*. Retrieved March 8, 2012, from washingtonpost.com/business/economy/hedge-fund-billionaire: http://www.washingtonpost.com

Ip, G. (06-10-1998). Philadelphia Exchange to join Nasdaq, Amex. *Wall Street Journal*, C1, C17.

Karnitschnig, M. S. (2008, September, 17). *U.S. to Take Over AIG in $85 Billion Bailout*. Retrieved January 12, 2012, from Online Wall Street Journal: http://online.wsj.com/article/SB122156561931242905.html

Kendall, B. (December 9, 2011). Wells settles Wachovia Big-Rig Case. *The Wall Street Journal*, C3.

Lohse, D. (1998). Frank G. Zarb! Duking It Out With Big Board. *The Wall Street Journal*, C1-C23 Column 1.

Lucchetti, A. (2011, November 15). *LCH Clearnet Finishes Unloading Corzine's European Bet*. Retrieved December 25, 2011, from Wall Street Journal: http://blogs.wsj.com/deals/2011/11/15/lch-clearnet-finishes-unloading-corzines-european . . .

Lucchetti, A. S. (01/17/2012). MF Probe Targets Back-Office Unit. *The Wall Street Journal*, C1-C2.

Patterson, S. L. (12/09/2011). Ex—CEO Deflects Blame for Failure, Says He's Puzzled Over Missing Funds. *The Wall Street Journal*, C1—C2.

Rappaport, & Enrich. (March 15, 2012). Goldman Plays Damage Control. *The Wall Street Journal*, C1-C2.

Reporter, S. (1991). Keating is told by SEC He faces being Charged. *The Wall Street Journal*, F8—B4:6.

Reporter, S. (March 19,1991). Milkens agree to SEC Ban From Securities for Lifetime. *The Wall Street Journal*, A4:4.

Reynolds, L. (1991, June). Holding Accountants Accountable. *Washington Perspective / Management Review*, pp. 36-37.

Rothfeld, M. Z. (02/10/2012). Insider Bill Passes with New Backers. *The Wall Street Journal*, C1-C2.

Scannell, K. (2009, May 16). *Insider Trading Probe at SEC*. Retrieved July 4, 2012, from Wall Street Journal Website: http://online.wsj.com/article/SB124241028545124563.html

Shapiro, S. P. (1984). *Wayward Capitalists*. Yale University Press.

Smith, R. a. (03-15-2012). SEC Cracks Down On Pre-IPO Trading. *The Wall Street Journal*, A1-A2.

Sparshott, J. (April 05, 2012). Regions Returns TARP Money. *The Wall Street Journal*, C3.

Timiraos, N. B. (12/17-18/2011). SEC Brings Crisis-Era Suits. *The Wall Street Journal*, B1-B2.

Wikipedia. (2008). *Automotive Industry Crisis of 2008-2010*. Retrieved August 13, 2012, from Wikipedia: http://en.wikipedia.org/wiki/Automotive_industry_crisis_of_2008%E2%80%932010

Wikipedia. (2011, October 11). *Enron*. Retrieved October 11, 2011, from Wikipedia, the free encyclopedia: http://en.wikipedia.org/wiki/Enron_scandal

Wikipedia. (2011). *Troubled Asset Relief Program*. Retrieved August 13, 2012, from Wikipedia: http://en.wikipedia.org/wiki/Troubled_Asset_Relief_Program

Wikipedia. (2012). *Allen Stanford*. Retrieved July 4, 2012, from Wikipedia: http://en.wikipedia.org/wiki/ Allen_Stanford

Wikipedia. (2012). *Jamie Dimon*. Retrieved July 4, 2012, from Wikipedia: http://en.wikipedia.org/wiki/Jamie_Diamon

Wikipedia. (2012). *Libor*. Retrieved August 1, 2012, from Wikipedia: http://en.wikipedia.org/wiki/Libor_scandal

Wikipedia. (2012). *Raj Rajaratnam*. Retrieved March 31, 2012, from Wikipedia: http://www.wikipedia.org/wiki/Raj_Rajaratnam

Wikipedia. (2012, March 25). *Rajat Gupta*. Retrieved March 25, 2012, from Wikipedia.org: wikipedia.org/wiki/Rajat_Gupta

Wikipedia. (2012). *Solyndra*. Retrieved July 1, 2012, from Wikipedia: http://en.wikipedia.org/wiki/Solyndra_loan_controversy

Wikipedia. (n.d.). *American International Group*. Retrieved July 1, 2012, from Wikipedia: http://en.wikipedia.org/wiki/American_International_Group

Wikipedia. (n.d.). *American Stock Exchange*. Retrieved January 6, 2012, from Wikipedia.Org: http://en.wikipedia.org/wiki/American_Stock_Exchange

Wikipedia. (n.d.). *Anil Kumar*. Retrieved March 25, 2012, from Wikipedia: http://www.wikipedia.org/wiki/Anil_Kumar_(businessman)

Wikipedia. (n.d.). *Enron Scandal*. Retrieved October 11th., 2011, from Wikipedia: http://en.wikipedia.org/wiki/Enron

Wikipedia. (n.d.). *Federal Reserve System*. Retrieved April 3, 2012, from Wikipedia: httn://en.wikipedia.org/wiki/Federal_Reserve_System

Wikipedia. (n.d.). *Insider Trading*. Retrieved June 18, 2012, from Wikipedia: http://en.wikipedia.org/wiki/Insider_trading

Wikipedia. (n.d.). *Lehman Brothers*. Retrieved July 2, 2012, from Wikipedia: http://en.wikipedia.org/wiki/Lehman_Brothers

Wikipedia. (n.d.). *Madoff Investment Scandal*. Retrieved November 5, 2011, from Wikipedia, the free encyclopedia: http://en.wikipedia.org/wiki/Madoff_investment_scandal

Wikipedia. (n.d.). *MF Global*. Retrieved June 18, 2012, from Wikipedia: http://en.wikipedia.org/wiki/MF_Global

Wikipedia. (n.d.). *Michael Milken*. Retrieved November 25, 2011, from Wikipedia: http://en.wikipedia.org/wiki/Milken

Wikipedia. (n.d.). *NYSE Euronext, Inc*. Retrieved March 25, 2012, from Wikipedia.org: http://en.wikipedia.org/wiki/NYSE_Euronext

Wikipedia. (n.d.). *Tom Petters*. Retrieved March 25, 2012, from Wikipedia: http://en.wikipedia.org/wiki/Tom_Petters

Wikipedia, C. (n.d.). *Wikipedia*. Retrieved November 28th., 2011, from Wikipedia, the free encyclopedia: http://en.wikipedia.org/wiki/Ivan_Boesky

Index

A

Abelow, Bradley I., 111
Ahearn, Mike, 105
AICPA (American Institute of Certified Public Accountants), 53
AIG (American International Group), 56–57, 60, 74, 100–101
Albukerk, Lawrence, 65
Alpern, Saul, 86
AMEX (American Stock Exchange), 87
   black injustice at, 26
   communication systems, 19–20
   See also mark-sensed cards
   as a competitive SRO, 23, 149
   NASD and NYSE feud over, 140–48
   and NASD merger, 138–39
   parting of NASD and, 141–42
   religious liberty at, 33
   rules of, 22
   scandal investigations at, 136–37
   specialists of, 34
   supervisors on, 33
   system acronyms, 39
Amicus Trading, 122
Arthur Andersen LLP, 74–75
Ashmore Energy International Ltd., 75

B

Bacchus, Eustace, 21
banks, 106, 127
Bear Sterns Cos., 92, 100, 128
Berkeley, Alfred, 148
Berman, Douglas A., 115
Bernanke, Ben, 62, 99, 101
Bharara, Preet, 109, 114
Big Board. *See* NYSE (New York Stock Exchange)
Bingham McCutchen LLP, 129
Blankfein, Lloyd C., 67–68, 118
BLMIS (Bernard L. Madoff Investment Securities LLC), 85–86, 90–91
Bloom Staloff Corp., 145
Board of Governors, 45, 57
Boesky, Ivan Frederick, 74, 79–81, 115
Borsa Italiana, 151
Brodsky, William, 144
brokers
   curbstone, 15
   floor official, 33
Brown, Scott P., 64
Bush, George W., 56–58, 101

C

Cacioppi, Theodore, 90
Campbell, John, 63
CAT (consolidated audit trail), 131
CBO (Congressional Budget Office), 56, 59–60
CBOE (Chicago Board of Options Exchange), 87, 143–44
CFTC (Commodity Futures Trading Commission), 109
Cheung, Meaghan, 89
Chin, Denny, 92
Cicilline, David, 64
Citigroup Inc., 56, 59, 77–78, 127
Cohn, Gary D., 67–68
Coleman, Deanna, 124–25
Congress, 44, 51, 137
  authorizing TARP, 60
  and insider trading, 63–64
  and the jobs bill, 64
  members of, 49, 62–63, 69, 99
COP (Congressional Oversight Panel), 59
Corzine, Jon S., 74, 108–13
Cotchett, Joseph, 92
Coughlin Stoia Geller Rudman and Robbins, 77
Cox, Christopher, 151
CPP (Capital Purchase Program), 58

D

Daniel, Ron, 118
Deikel, Ted, 123
Delivery Concepts LLC, 92
Dellosso, Donna, 112
Den of Thieves (Stewart), 81
Deutsche Borse, 150–51
Dewey, Tom, 90
Division of Enforcement, 41
Division of Trading and Exchanges, 42, 136
DK Room, 20
Dodd, Christopher, 58
Dow Jones & Co., 147
Dow Jones Industrial Average, 98, 101, 131
Drexel Burnham Lambert Inc., 79–80
Duffy, Sean, 64
Dynegy, 75

E

Ear Electronics, 122
EB Financial Group LLC, 65
Ellis (Judge), 91
Emergency Economic Stabilization Act of 2008, 57
Energy Conversion Devices Inc., 105
Enron Corporation, 74–75
Enron Creditors Recovery Corp. *See* Enron Corporation
exchange specialists, 35

F

Facebook IPO, 64–67
Facie Libre Management Associates LLC, 65
Fagel, Marc, 64
Falcone, Philip, 74, 96–97
Fannie Mae, 56, 100, 125
Fastow, Andrew, 75–77
Fastow, Lea, 76
FBI (Federal Bureau of Investigation)
  and the arrest of Gupta, 116–17, 121
  and the arrest of Madoff, 90
  and the arrest of Rajaratnam, 113
  and the investigation of MF Global, 109, 111
  and the investigation of Petters, 123

FCC (Federal Communications Commission), 97
FCRA (Federal Credit Reform Act), 59
FDIC (Federal Deposit Insurance Corporation), 49, 125
Federal Reserve Act, 44, 100
Federal Reserve Board. *See* Board of Governors
Federal Reserve System, 44–46, 57, 115, 155
FHLMC (Federal Home Loan Mortgage Corporation). *See* Freddie Mac
Fineman, Nancy, 92
Fingerhut Companies Inc., 123
FINRA (Financial Industry Regulatory Authority), 65–66, 94, 131–32, 152
First Solar Inc., 105
Fitzgerald, Patrick, 109
Flumenbaum, Martin, 90
FNMA (Federal National Mortgage Association). *See* Fannie Mae
FOMC (Federal Open Market Committee), 45
fraud
  of Anil Kumar, 120–22
  of Bernard Madoff, 93
  cases, 74
  of Charles H. Keating, Jr., 79
  Citicorp charges of, 78
  Enron Corporation, 74–77
  financial, 50, 52
  of Ivan Boesky, 81
  of Jon Corzine, 113
  of Rajat Gupta, 116–20
  of Raj Rajaratnam, 113–16
  of Tom Petters, 125
  of Wells Fargo Bank, 96
Freddie Mac, 56, 100, 125–27
funds
  hedge, 114, 128–30
  money-market, 101

private-equity, 129–30

G

Galleon Management, 114
Geithner, Tim, 58
General Accounting Office, 51, 59
German Stock Market. *See* Deutsche Borse
Giddens, James, 109
Gilder, George, 80
  Telocosm, 80
Goldman Sachs Group Inc., 65, 67–68, 127
Grassley, Charles, 97
Grasso, Richard, 145–46
Guinness, Jonathan, 81
  Requiem for a Family Business, 81
Gupta, Rajat Kumar, 116

H

Harbinger Capital Partners LLC, 97
Hardiman, Joseph, 145
Healy, Patrick, 131
Heis, Richard, 108
Hewitt, Jack, 65
Holwell, Richard J., 114
House of Representatives, 46, 49, 62

I

immigrant injustices, 69
insider trading. *See* Stock Act
IPO (initial public offering), 64, 105
Issuer Advisory Group LLC, 131

J

Jacobs, John, 52
jobs bill, 64, 66

J. P. Morgan Chase & Co., 112–13
Junk Bond King. *See* Milken, Michael Robert
junk bonds, 80

K

Kaitz, Jim, 51, 53
Kaplan, Robert, 129–30
Kapur, Chetan, 130
Karpati, Bruce, 129–30
Keating, Charles H., Jr., 74, 79
Ketchum, Richard, 143, 146
Khuzami, Robert, 125, 127, 129
Krishnan, Lata, 116
Kumar, Anil, 116, 118–21

L

Lake, Sim, 76
Lay, Kenneth, 75–76
Lay, Linda, 76
LCH Clearnet, 108
Lehman Brothers Holding Inc., 100–101, 126
Leonard, Robert, 129
Levine, Dennis, 74, 80
Lieberman, Sam, 130
LightSquared Inc., 97–98
Lincoln Savings and Loan Association, 79
Lower Manhattan Plaza. *See* Zuccotti Park

M

Madakasira, Pallavi, 106
Madoff, Bernard L., 73–74, 85–93, 129–30
Madoff, Ruth, 90, 92
Madoff Securities International Ltd., 87–88, 90–91, 93

market
 auction, 19, 146
 dealer, 146
 investors of public, 105
 private-shares, 64
 secondary, 64
marketplace, 110. *See also* AMEX (American Stock Exchange)
market surveillance analysts, 23
Markopolos, Harry, 89
mark-sensed cards, 38
Martens, Matthew T., 78
Massad, Tim, 60
Mazzola, Frank, 65
Menezes, Victor, 116
Merrill Lynch & Co., 101
MF Global Holdings, 74, 107–13
Milan Stock Exchange. *See* Borsa Italiana
Milken, Lowell, 79
Milken, Michael Robert, 79–81
Miller, Paul, 126
Moragilo, Joe, 53
Mudd, Daniel, 125–26
Muppets, 68

N

Naftalis, Gary, 119
NASD (National Association of Securities Dealers), 86
 deal of, 140, 148
 feud with NYSE, 145–48
 on merger with AMEX, 138
 parting with AMEX, 142
 on Philadelphia Stock Exchange deal, 143, 145
 tentative agreement with AMEX, 139–40
NASD-AMEX, merger, 137–40, 143

NASDAQ (National Association of Securities Dealers Automated Quotations), 142
  on merger with AMEX, 138–39
  planned international deals, 147
  view of, 145
Nasdaq Stock Market, 138, 143, 145
National Securities Markets Improvement Act of 1996, 23
Neal, Stephen C., 79
New Silk Route, 116, 121
New York Curb Market, 15, 23. *See also* AMEX (American Stock Exchange)
9/11, 22
Nyppex Holdings LLC, 64
NYSE (New York Stock Exchange), 15, 23
  bane of, 86
NYSE Euronext, plan to acquire AMEX, 142, 150–52

O

Obama, Barack, 63, 127
  administration, 58
O'Brien, Edith, 112–13
Occupy Wall Street, 69–70, 74
OPM (Option Principal Member), 35, 141
OptiMark, 147–48
options
  buyer, 35
  contract, 35
  trading, 33, 139
Osborne, Jeff, 105

P

Pacific Exchange, 144
Pascuma, Michael J., Jr., 21
Pascuma, Michael J., Sr., 21

Paulson, Henry, 57–58, 100–101
Petters, Thomas Joseph, 122–25
Petters Company. *See* Amicus Trading
Petters Group Worldwide, 122–24
Petters Warehouse Direct, 122
Philadelphia Stock Exchange, 143–44
Political Profiles, 52
Ponzi scheme. *See* Madoff, Bernard L.
Price, Kenneth, 77
Primex Holdings LLC, 93
Prisma Energy International Inc., 75
Proctor & Gamble, 119

R

Rajaratnam, Raj, 113, 116–18, 121
Rakoff, Jed S., 77–78
Rangnekar, Ajit, 120
Ratley, James, 89
Regions Financial Corp., 60
reporters, 31
Requiem for a Family Business (Guinness), 81
Richman, Daniel, 98
Rosenberg, Barr, 98

S

Salmon, Walter J., 118
Sarbanes-Oxley Act of 2002, 74
scandal
  Enron, 73–77, 116
  Madoff investment, 85, 93, 155
  Valhalla. *See* scandal, Enron
Schapiro, Mary, 66, 131, 145, 147
Scheehan, David, 88
Scott, Robert C., 63
SEC (Securities and Exchange Commission), 40–41
  administrative proceeding of, 44
  authority on investigative work, 42

easing reporting for audits of trading, 132
investigating AMEX and NYSE, 73
investigation on Enron, 75
investigation on Madoff, 86, 88
reputation of, 43
on SRO fees, 23
sueing Gupta, 116
upping game to find rogue firms, 128–30
self-regulation, 23
Senate, 58
Serwinski, Christine, 113
Shi, Zhengrong, 105
SIFMA (Securities Industry and Financial Markets), 88
Skilling, Jeffrey, 75–77, 115–16
Slaughter, Louise M., 64
Smith, Greg, 67
snowballs, 76
Sodano, Salvatore F., 141
solar
  industry, 104
  panels, 103–4, 106
  power, 104, 106
Solyndra, 74, 102–5, 155
Sommers, Jill, 109
SRO (Self-Regulatory Organization), 22
Staloff, Arnold, 145
Stanton, Lewis, 92
Steenkamp, Henri J., 111
Sterling Equities, 92
Stewart, James B., 81
Den of Thieves, 81
Stock Act, 62–63
stock cards. *See* mark-sensed cards
stock market, agencies that influence, 40–53
Stock Option, 35, 144
stocks, 34
Stop Trading on Congressional Knowledge Act. *See* Stock Act
Sun Country Airlines, 123–24
Sun-Tech Power Holdings Co., 105
Susman, Harry, 89
Syron, Richard F., 141
  case against, 126
  on deal with Philadelphia Stock Exchange, 144
  on NASD deal, 140

T

TARP (Troubled Asset Relief Program), 56–60
Telecosm (Gilder), 80
Thain, John, 151
Theodore, Jean-Francois, 151
ThinkStrategy Capital Management LLP, 130
traders, 32, 141, 145, 147
trading
  business of, 19
  equity, 139
  floor, 17, 20, 138, 142
  posts, 17
  rules of, 22
Treadway Commission, 52

U

UC (University of California), 77

V

Vavra, Christy, 113
Vennes, Frank, 125

W

Wachovia Bank, 96
Wallace, John F., 143–44
Wall Street, 69, 73, 100, 127–28
Wells Fargo & Co., 96
Wells notices, 127
whistle-blowers, 29, 68
White, Robert Dean, 124
Willumstad, Robert, 100
Wolff, Max, 65
Woodall, Rob, 63
WTC (World Trade Center), 21
Wyden, Ron, 50–53
Wyden bill, 51–52

Z

Zarb, Frank G., 140–41, 145–47
Ziman, Kenneth S., 109
Zuccotti Park, 69–70